Understanding Network Activity: The Role of IP Traffic Identification

Chris

Table of Contents

1 INTRODUCTION

1.1 5G Slicing and Management

1.1.1 Internet Protocol (IP) Traffic Rise

Identification of IP traffic is important in the network management and network security domain. For network operators, traffic identification helps to provide better network services, such as traffic accounting and optimizing the allocation of network resources. Security managers are required to identify abnormal IP traffic patterns and data for network security. For application developers, it is necessary to know the application usage so that they can improve their product.

With the introduction of 4th Generation (4G) Long Term Evolution (LTE) technology and because of its availability, many devices which are capable of accessing the Internet have been developed all over the world. For example, various types of cell phones, tablets, laptops, IoT (Internet of Things) devices and autonomous drones. With these different devices, people who are accessing the Internet have affected Internet traffic management systems. The exponential growth of Internet applications has introduced new challenges when it comes to network management. Figure 1-1 shows predicted connected devices in billions over years. Graph shows how 4G has increased modern-day Internet connections. Thus, a similar growth of connected devices can be expected for 5th Generation (5G).

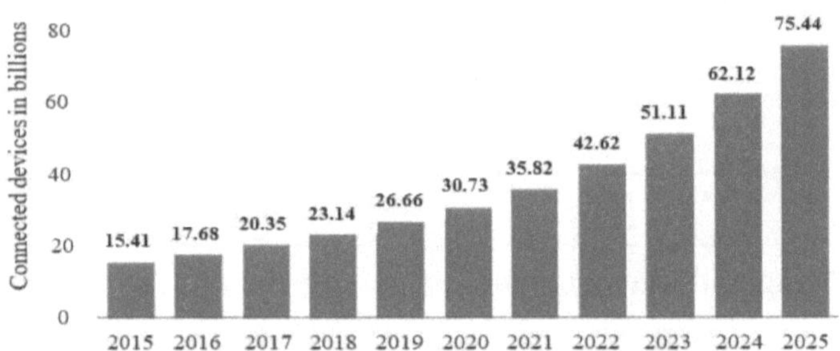

Figure 1-1: Usage of Internet Connections over Time [1]

It is clear that more connections mean more internet traffic and hence more data traffic. Another report generated by Statistica (Figure 1-2) shows that the number of available apps in the Google Play Store has already exceeded 2500K in March 2019, up from 16K in December 2009 [1]. Thus, about 157 times more apps have been developed within 10 years. If this trend continues in coming years, one can imagine the data packet traffic generated by all connections in the world.

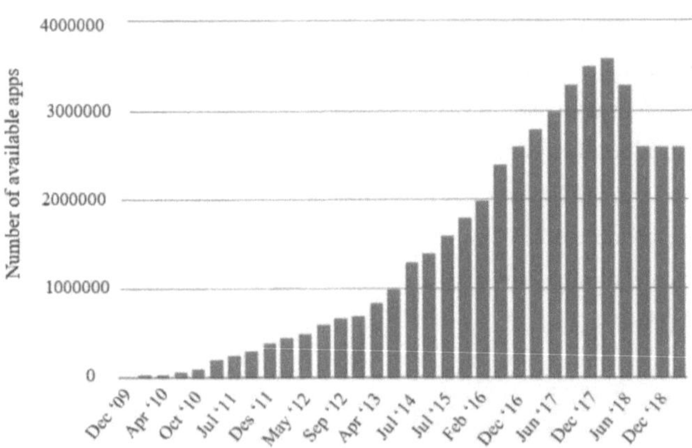

Figure 1-2: Google App Store Downloads [1]

To accommodate ever-growing internet connections and the public's hunger for data, it is identified that the network should be an agile, automatic, and intelligent during each phase of the network architecture. Therefore, a need for a 5th generation network arises.

1.1.2 Beginning of 5G

Researchers all around the globe started to develop 5th generation networks due to huge demand in the market. Researches in various nations around the world formed their own fora to come up with their solutions. Namely, mobile and wireless communications enablers for the Twenty-twenty Information Society (METIS) [2], Next Generation Mobile Network (NGMN) [3] , 5G Infrastructure Public Private Partnership (5GPPP) [4] in Europe, 4G/5G Americas in U.S. [5], 5G Forum in Korea, and International Mobile Telecommunications-2020 (IMT-2020) [6] in China.

Fifth Generation Mobile Communication Promotion Forum (5GMF) [7] was established by the Japanese to set a research path for 5G in Japan. 5GMF network architecture committee released a whitepaper in 2016, mentioning key concepts in 5G mobile networks such as supporting extremely flexible communication infrastructure to maintain end-to-end quality of applications for different requirements. 5GMF network architecture committee found that key technical requirements to achieving end-to-end quality of service (QoS) are network softwarisation and slicing, mobile edge computing (MEC), mobile front-haul technologies, network management and orchestration.

ITU-T [8] decided to form a focus group called IMT-2020 in 2015. IMT-2020 realised that emerging 5G technologies should be future proofed. Thus should interact well with future networks. Hence, a preliminary study was conducted by the IMT-2020 group on networking innovations required to support the development of 5G systems. They have paid attention to fundamental issues that need to be addressed when designing 5G networks. The IMT-2020 committee recommended some of the high-level capabilities and characteristics that should be supported by future networks (FNs). They also conducted research to find the gap between network technologies and advanced technical concepts such as network softwarisation and network slicing, and information centric networking in 5G mobile networking [9]. Thus new devices which can support network slicing will be deployed in the RAN networks.

In the meantime, Huawei released a white paper [10] based on their views. Huawei thinks of the 5G network as a single network infrastructure which can support various types of services. Throughout the paper, researchers of Huawei discuss about a Cloud-Native End-to-End (E2E) network architecture. Huawei identifies that the following features should be in a 5G network:

1. Provides logically independent network slicing on a single network infrastructure to meet diversified service requirements and provides data centre (DC) based cloud architecture to support various application scenarios.
2. Uses CloudRAN to reconstruct radio access networks (RAN) to provide massive connections of multiple standards and implement on-demand deployment of RAN functions required by 5G.
3. Simplifies the core network architecture to implement on demand configuration of network functions through control and user plane separation, component-based functions, and unified database management.
4. Implements automatic network slicing service generation, maintenance, and termination for various services to reduce operating expenses through agile network operation and maintenance.

If one goes through all the above-mentioned reports, it is clear that all the research discuss network slicing as one of the main features of 5G network. The concept of network slicing has been used in this study; therefore, it is important to have a general idea of network slicing.

1.1.3 Introduction to 5G Slicing

In simple terms 5G slicing is allocating resources in the 5G network in order to give the desired Quality of Service (QoS) for the user or for the application. In the modern world all sort of things have connections to the core network. Machines such as drones, automated cars, medical equipment, etc. need to access and get data with minimum possible time, and hence are time dependent. There are things such as mobile phones, tablets, dongles, etc. which are used to connect by the general public, therefore in massive numbers. They need to have a good data speed to watch videos, to chat, to play games, etc. Then, there are sensors with internet connections to collect data. These types of connections can be found in automated factories, on the street, in smart homes, etc.

and these type of connections don't connect to internet all the time but the number of devices are extravagant compared to devices used by general public. After studying various requirements, all the standardisation organizations mentioned in the previous section (1.1.3) started to group devices based on their QoS requirements.

The 5GMNF white paper classifies communications to be enabled in 5G mobile networking into three categories: eMBB (enhanced Mobile Broadband), URLLC (Ultra Reliable and Low Latency Communication) and mMTC (massive Machine Type Communication). Similarly, the 5G Infrastructure Public Private Partnership (5G PPP) defined three main use case in 5G network. Namely, mMTC also known as massive Internet of Things (mIoT) targeted to connect immobile sensors and machines, XMBB (Massive Broad Band) to deliver gigabytes of bandwidth to mobile devices on demand and uMTC (ultra-reliable machine-type communication) to allow immediate feedback with high reliability in case like autonomous driving and remote controlled robots [11]. Although the terminologies are different, these three categories of communications defined by the 5GMNF and 5G PPP organizations imply that 5G mobile networks must support very different quality of service (QoS) for each type of communications as shown in Figure 1-3. Thus 5G mobile networks should addresses the requirements for supporting extreme flexibility in 5G mobile networks.

5G Use Cases	Examples	Requirements	Mobility
eMBB/xMBB	4K/8K ultra high definition (UHD) video, hologram, Augmented Reality (AR), Virtual Reality (VR)	High capacity, video cache	Yes
mMTC	Sensor Networks (smart metering, logistics, city, home, etc.)	Massive connection covering a very large area of mostly immobile devices	No
URLLC/uMTC	Autonomous driving, smart-grid, remote surgery	Low latency and high reliability	Yes

Figure 1-3: Main 5G Slices [11]

ITU considered the above mentioned example situations and introduced their idea of the 5G slicing ecosystem as shown in Figure 1-4. eMBB devices will connect to a 10Gbps link and uRLLC will connect to a link which has a 1ms of latency and the mMTC devices will connect to a link which can handle 1million/km^2 connections. Three main slices for three main categories are expected in the core network for the 5G ecosystem. However the number of slices has not been standardized by the ITU committee at the time of writing this.

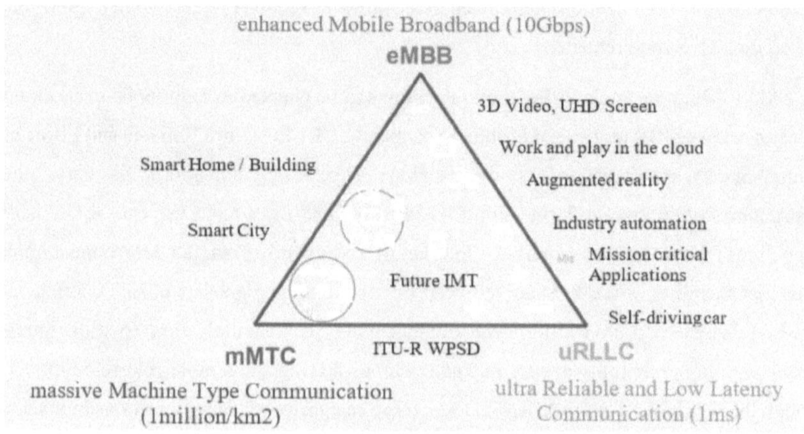

Figure 1-4: ITU-R 5G Slicing Triangle [8]

1.1.4 End-to-End Slicing

Years of research on network virtualisation and software-defined networking has enabled end-to-end network slicing. Although the end-to-end slicing via network virtualisation is new to mobile network ecosystem, companies like Huawei are making rapid progress due to resent semiconductor technologies. Fifth Generation Mobile Communication Promotion Forum (5GMF) [12] also recognize the importance of End-to-End slicing. 5GMF have defined End-to-End network slicing all the way from user equipment (UE) to cloud data centres to establish a virtually separated network connection which can run various applications. The Figure 1-5 shows a block diagram of proposed architecture.

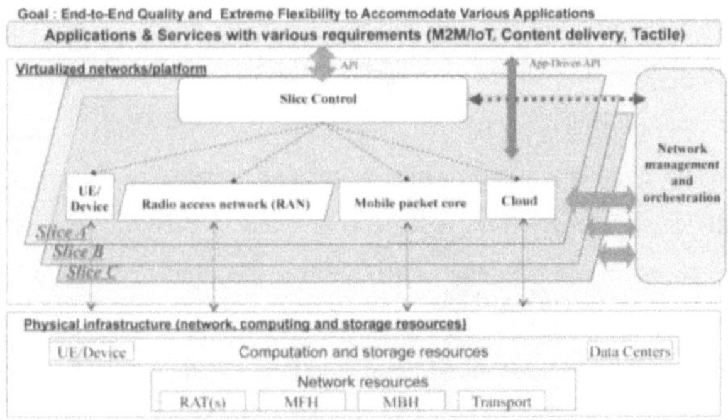

Figure 1-5: End-to-End Slicing Network Architecture [7] [11]

Figure 1-5 also depicts the main aspects of network slicing physical infrastructure, virtualized networks and network management and orchestration. The physical infrastructure shows a collection of networks, devices and storage resources which connects to core network. Thus End-to-End slicing should be able to provide slices to the equipment in the physical infrastructure. Thus the 5G network should be able to deploy slices between user equipment (UE) and cloud data centres by using programmable resources for every application that require a slice. To achieve slicing, the network will dynamically create, modify and destroy network slices across the fixed networks and radio boundary, namely radio access network (RAN) slicing and mobile core slicing.

1.2 Problem Formulation

According to 5G white papers and studies conducted by various research groups, it is clear that in the near future there will be 5G slices and the network orchestrator will decide to deploy, destroy or modifying the slices, based on connections and applications. However, End-to-End slicing would be applied to a device or for a set of devices which is not the ideal case. In this study, we focused on the eMBB slice. Even in the eMBB slice, it is expected to have many application types. However, some applications need to be prioritized over others in some scenarios. For example,

- A family doctor may give first aid assistance via a Skype video call in an emergency situation. Thus the Skype video call of the doctor, in this case, should be prioritized over other normal daily web tasks.

- Let's take another situation where there is a separate slice for universities, all the PCs of students, teachers, etc. will be connected to this slice. Thus all the university connections would have the same QoS even though some might be watch Facebook movies while some students trying to study via LinkedIn videos. Clearly reducing the bandwidth of Facebook video would help the students who are trying to study. A researcher might use the internet connection to download data from a cloud service while someone else is downloading a TV series. But the 5G Orchestrator would not be able to distinguish a researcher downloading data for that person's research (which should have higher priority over downloading TV series). This would result in providing the same bandwidth all the time.

- In a situation where there is a network failure, some important web tasks shouldn't be disturbed because of an overwhelming number of connections.

In the current eMBB slice it is not possible to detect such scenarios; thus, there is an issue of prioritizing a web-task in such situations. Hence, the authors of this study recognise the need for web application task slicing and orchestration in 5G mobile core networks. The proposed solution is explained in the following section.

1.3 Proposed Solution

The authors of this study, propose to identify the web task and develop slices within slices (Ultra-slices) to get the maximum use of network slicing concept, thus get the optimum resources usage for the 5G ecosystem. Presently, 5G slices are developed for the equipment (could be an edge database, gateway, router, etc.). Users who use the network might use it for various things thus it is necessary to know what the user is doing at the present moment. Then resources can be allocated for the user based on the user's web usage.

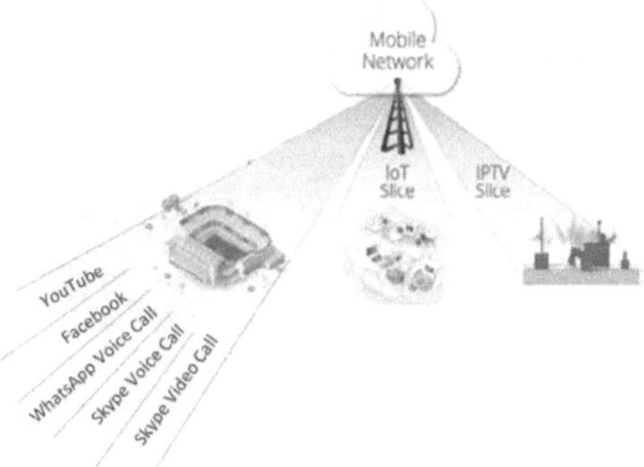

Figure 1-6 : Web-task Slices

In this study, the authors recognise the web task and not just the website. Detecting web tasks is different from detecting websites, for example, a user might log into his skype account and might chat, voice call or video chat. Thus, it is important to know what that person is doing at that moment because the QoS differs for each of the web tasks mentioned. For example Skype chat require less bandwidth compared to Skype video chat. Thus allocating same bandwidth for Skype chat and Skype video chat is a waste of resources. Henceforth it is clear that extravagant resources usage can be stopped by detecting the web task rather than detecting the website.

In this study five common web tasks were chosen to develop 5G slices namely; Facebook videos, YouTube videos, Skype voice calls, Skype video calls and finally WhatsApp voice calls. However, the algorithm can be used to detect other web tasks as long as it is possible to get features as discussed in this study. The websites mentioned above were chosen carefully to prove the algorithm's robustness. In other words, three video related web-tasks and two audio related web-tasks were chosen for classification. Two similar websites from the same category (such as Facebook videos and YouTube videos) were chosen to conceptualise the power of the proposed algorithm. Identifying Skype voice calls and WhatsApp voice calls shows that the proposed algorithm is capable of differentiating voice from video as well as different protocols. Finally, differentiating Skype calls as video and voice shows its ability to separate web-tasks belonging to the same website. These captured features were then fed into a Neural Network-based classifier to identify the web task.

The inbound and outbound data was captured (as illustrated in Figure 1-7) from user equipment to detect web tasks. Figure 1-8 And Figure 1-9 respectively shows a sniffed packet rate graph of a Facebook video watching and YouTube video watching.

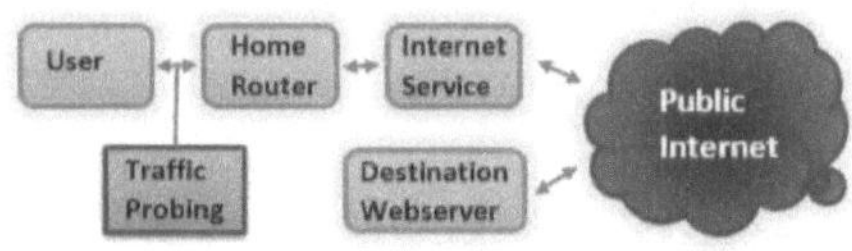

Figure 1-7: General Network Arrangement

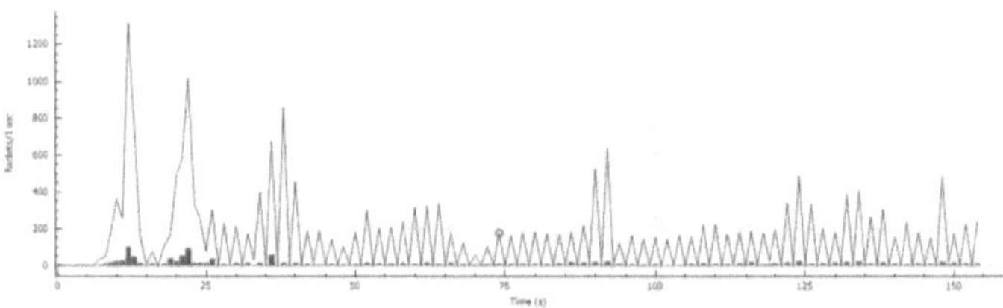

Figure 1-8: Facebook Video Watching

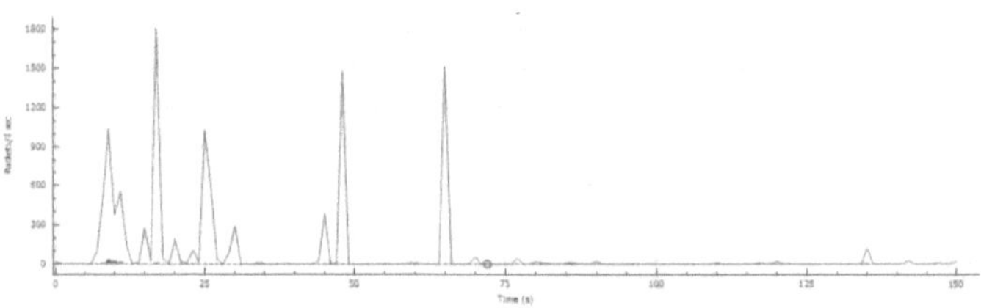

Figure 1-9: YouTube Video Watching

According to Figure 1-8 and Figure 1-9, it is clear that Facebook and YouTube videos have entirely different packet rate patterns. By scrutinizing the graphs, one can understand that YouTube generates data in short sporadic intervals and waits a while before sending the next chunk of data. On the other hand, Facebook continually sends a small number of bytes per second. It is clear that websites have different fingerprints for achieving the same task (in this case streaming video). Based on Related work (Chapter 2) packet lengths were chosen to identify these different packet rate patterns. A unique set of features were extracted for each website task based on data rate patterns.

After extracting features various types of Artificial Intelligent (AI) algorithms were used to find a proper algorithm. Authors of this study have considered four different Machine Learning (ML) algorithms to find the best algorithm. The considered algorithms are Multi-layer Perceptron (MLP) based Artificial Neural Network (ANN), Support Vector Machine (SVM), Recurrent Neural Network (RNN) and Convolutional Neural Network (CNN). These extracted features were fed to find the best hypo parameters and variables for each AI algorithm. Then best ML algorithm was chosen by comparing the accuracy of each algorithm.

Next, the classifier results were used by both 5G orchestrator and 5G Core to orchestrate and deploy slices for each web task. The Open Baton [13] 5G orchestrator was chosen as the 5G orchestrator for this study. Open Baton is an open-source platform providing a comprehensive implementation of the ETSI Network Function Virtualization (NFV) Management and Orchestration (MANO) specification. Open Baton is able to orchestrate resources within an OpenStack based Virtualized Infrastructure Manager (VIM) for the creation and enforcement of the relevant 5G network slices through its Network Slicing Engine and Auto Scaling Engine. Hence Open Baton was used to allocate the necessary QoS (ultra-slices) for the detected applications. Then 5G core was used to further experiment the concept of ultra-slicing.

1.4 Research Contributions

The contributions of this work can be summarized as follows:

- Thorough data analysis on IP data packets.

- Encryption and protocol-independent feature extraction within 5 seconds of data flow.

- Comparison between MLP, CNN, RNN and SVM classification algorithms.

- Traffic can be classified into the correct task and belonging to the correct website with 95.50% accuracy.

- Developing network slices for detected web task by a 5G network orchestrator and 5G Core.

(Published papers were given in the Appendix 4)

1.5 Objectives

To solve the issue pointed out in the previous section, the following objectives were achieved:

- Detecting web task
  - Extract unique features for web tasks
  - Selection of a suitable classifier

- Using a 5G orchestrator and Open5G Core to developing network slices
  - Establish a communication between the classifier and 5G the orchestrator
  - Deploy slices on the 5G testbed

1.6 Scope and Limitations

The scope of this book is limited to developing a web-task classifier and then using it to develop a 5G network slice.   Developing a web-task classifier was inspired by website classification algorithms. Website classifications were developed by researchers for many years, thus there are many ways to develop web task classifier. However, an ethical way of developing web task classifier was proposed by this book. Thus avoided utilising mechanisms such as deep packet inspection.

Although the web task classifier is similar to Website classifiers, the purpose of these two is different. In this book , the web task classifier was developed with the intention of providing a slice (upon user request) for the user device just for the period of accessing a specific web task.

Thus classifying all the web tasks is not the scope of this book. Thus the main scope of web task classifier is to develop a method which can be used to classify web task upon request. However, five web tasks have been classified in this book for the demonstration. The data pattern for the same web-task will change in different parts of the country. However, collecting data in deferent parts of the country is time-consuming and it requires a higher budget. Thus this study is focused within west Cape Town.

5G orchestration and 5G core algorithms are still under research. Thus deploying slices is a hot topic in the 5G research field. However, the issues of 5G slicing such as time taking to deploy, destroy or switching were not part of this book. Although theoretically, it is possible to create many slices in practical it might be limited due to computation power available in the area. Similarly, the lab equipment available for the experiment limits the number of slices that can be developed in the lab. Thus, only one slice with auto-scaling has developed in this book.

1.7   book Outline

Remaining chapters of the book is structured as follows:

Chapter 2: provides a summary of related work that has been published related to this book. This section was separated into two main categories. Firstly, papers related to website identification is presented. This provides a background of features that have been used, conditions that might matter and algorithms that have been used to classify websites. Secondly, papers related to 5G orchestration and the 5G Core are presented to find out different use cases and to understand the concepts.

Chapter 3: provides a data analysis that has been conducted to understand and find proper features. In this section, a main feature was recognized. Then normalizing and visualization was done to study about packet behaviour on the internet. Then certain data patterns were recognized for each web task. Next, based on patterns few equations have been identified to extract web task-related features.

Chapter4: this chapter is focused on the theory behind AI algorithms. Four different AI algorithms were discussed in Chapter 4. Namely, Support Vector Machines (SVM), Multi-layer Perceptron (MLP), Convolutional Neural Networks (CNN) and Recurrent Neural Network (RNN). Parameters of each algorithm were discussed in this section. Explained parameters were used to experiment in the Chapter 5.

Chapter 5: describes the way web task classifier that was built. This chapter shows the pre-processing, feature extraction and classification. The pre-processing section is about how the algorithm is sniffing and filtering data. The feature extraction section shows how to apply the equations that have been identified in Chapter 3 to extract features. Then the classification section describes how the best performing AI algorithm was selected with an introduction to hyper parameters.

Chapter 6: explains the implementation of the testbed for experiments. This section also explains the main components of Open5G Core and 5G orchestrator. This is followed by the executed codes for the experiments.

Chapter 7: The results are discussed in this section. Firstly, the steps that have taken are explained. Then results observed from the testbed setup are explained with respect to step taken.

Chapter 8: Finally the conclusions, a small summary and future work are discussed in Chapter 8.

2 RELATED WORK

Identifying websites from IP data packets was well studied in the past. However, it is still a hot topic due to its importance, and various models were designed to address the diverse and changing needs of different application scenarios. Mainly, recent technological developments in communications such as encryption and port obfuscation have made it more difficult for researchers to classify websites and web tasks. Identifying websites is slightly different from identifying web-tasks (which is required for this book work) but studying website classification helps to develop a good web-task classifier. Website classification can be separated into three main categories according to work done by previous researchers.

1) Port-based methods
2) Payload-based methods
3) Statistical based methods

2.1 Port-based Methods

Port-based methods use the port number of the data packet to identify the website. Many applications today, for scalability, build their APIs (Application programming interfaces) on top of Content Distribution Networks (CDNs) such as Amazon AWS [14] or Microsoft Azure. This reduces (on average) the number of endpoints that applications communicate with. In the past, it may have been useful to look at the destination IP address or the port number of some IP traffic and infer the application that was sending the traffic. With the advent of CDNs and standard web service APIs, more applications are sending their traffic to similar endpoints, and this frustrates attempts to identify the website or application by using port-based methods. Despite all of this, a port number does not provide any useful information about a web-task, which is what the authors of this book are concerned about.

2.2 Payload-based Methods

Payload-based methods decode the IP data packet and use the information within the IP packet. This is also known as Deep Packet Inspection (DPI). DPI is one of the most famous payload based identification methods when it comes to packet inspection. For example, when requesting a web page, a browser will usually fetch the HTML document [15] and all corresponding resources identified by the HTML. Accessing this data to identify the website is DPI. If the traffic is unencrypted, DPI can be useful for traffic classification.

Bujlow et al. [16] perform an independent comparison of traffic classification tools that leverage on DPI. The researchers used six different DPI tools for the evaluation; two commercial tools (PACE and NBAR) and four open-source tools (OpenDPI, L7-filter, nDPI, and Libprotoident). The test data set was collected from various operating systems, namely, Windows XP, Windows 8 and Linux. They used a data set which included many different web applications such as using uTorrent (Windows), kTorrent (Linux), eMule (Windows), aMule (Linux), FileZilla (Windows, Linux) in active mode (PORT) and passive mode (PASV), Dropbox (Windows, Linux), 4Shared (+ Windows app), WebDAV (Windows), etc... First, 10 packets of each application were used to feed, to the DPI tools. The authors found that the PACE tool to be the best when considering performance. PACE was able to recognize Facebook (80.79%), Google (10.79%), Instagram (88.89%), Linkedin (77.42%), Mediafire (30.30%), Myspace (100%), QQ.com (32.14%), Twitter (71.18%), Windows Live (96.15%), Yahoo (54.70%), YouTube (81.97%) etc…. The results of PACE were good, especially because only 10 packets were used in identification, however, this research was conducted to identify web applications not web-tasks. Almost all the applications used in the experiment were downloading data from a server. Thus, the robustness of the DPI tools for uploading data is questionable. The authors have not conducted a real-time web application analysis.

Principle Component Analysis based DPI method combined with Web-site Finger Printing (WFP) algorithm was introduced by Garcia [17]. The research was focused only on video data traffic on cellular networks. Thus, classifying different video applications and detecting non-video background data packets are the main objectives of the research. This research uses statistical methods to classify data; hence the paper was explained under the statistical-based method section. Garcia agrees that DPI along cannot identify the encrypted data flows.

In addition to DPI's inability to classify encrypted data [18], it also raises ethical issues. Since some DPI algorithms look the data inside the packet payload there are issues regarding user data privacy. Thus, different approaches need to be taken when classifying data traffic.

2.3 Statistical based Methods

Statistical based methods uses the data on the wire, in other words, metadata generated by the IP packet data flow such as packet length, average bitrate, standard deviation, etc. as features to find websites.

A Statistical based Smartphone Application identifier was developed by Vincent et al. [19]. They were able to identify SSL/TLS protected mobile applications. Since this is a mobile application classifier the research was conducted by using a Motorola XT1039 phone with Android version 4.4.4 and an LG E960 phone with Android version 5.1.1. The researchers captured time, source address, destination address, ports, packet size, protocol and TCP/IP flags of each packet flowing in and out of the device. The dataset was created by using 110 applications from Google play store. Then authors used the flow area (the number of bits sent and received) as their main feature. Next, a portion of captured data was used to train a Random Forest classifier. They then tested the algorithm with near real-time data and were able to classify applications with a 96% accuracy. Since this algorithm was only focusing on mobile applications, the connection used was a Wi-Fi network since Ethernet is faster than Wi-Fi; it is not clear how the method used would work on a LAN connection. The authors only considering the android operating system (OS) thus unclear how it would function on an Apple device which has a different OS. The user was using the same network all the time even for the testing data; thus it is not clear how the network conditions would affect the accuracy.

A different approach was taken by Kampeas et al. [18], as they considered zero-length packets (e.g. ACK, SYN) as their main feature. The authors used virtual containers (Docker) for about 54 different web applications and websites. They considered the Application Protocol Data Units

(APDUs) patterns that occur between server and client in TCP communications. And similarly, the accumulated-APDU (a-APDU) pattern was considered for the UDP data packets. Although an application can create more than one APDU or a-APDU patterns two different applications would not create similar patterns. Thus, the authors classified web applications by recording and comparing these deferent patterns. The researchers were able to successfully classify with a 97% accuracy. The conditions concerned in this are totally different from the conditions concerned by this book research. Kampeas et al. wanted to run the algorithm inside the NFV and SDN setup. However, it is not clear how the algorithm conducted by Kampeas et al. would work when switching between different tasks such as Skype video calling to skype voice calling because both the web task were performed by the same application.

Work by Liberatore and Levine in [20] showed the feasibility of web-page identification via encrypted HTTP traffic analysis. The researchers considered OpenSSH implementation of a one-hop SOCKS proxy for the experiment. They used the direction and the length of packets as their main features. The experiment was conducted over 200 websites. The classification was done by using Jaccard's coefficient and Bayes classifiers. They recorded the data of each webpage beforehand and then by comparing stored data with online data by using Jaccard's coefficient and Bayes classifier, they managed to identify different websites. The authors experimented their algorithm with various parameters and managed to get a maximum of 88.9% of accuracy for Jaccard's coefficient method and 86.2% of accuracy with Bayes classifier. In this research, they used the same network and did not experimented with wireless networks. Since wireless networks data patterns are different from Ethernet it might generate a different data pattern. Thus, it is not clear how well the algorithm would work under these network conditions.

Hintz et al. [21] analyse the encrypted traffic of HTTP proxy servers that use SSL to encrypt their content. They show how an attacker can identify websites if that person is in possession of a library of their previously recorded "website fingerprints". The researchers captured data from a Windows machine by using the Explorer web browser. Packet length was considered as the feature. Then a packet length histogram was generated for the comparison. The authors was able to classify websites with 75% accuracy. The authors did not consider different types of networks, devices, connection types and classification methods. Although 75% of accuracy was achieved by the authors, the test set was also generated by using the same conditions. Thus, the reliability of the method was questionable.

Sun et al. [22] also researched on encrypted HTTP data. The authors presented evaluation results for a sample of 100,000 websites. They used packet length as their main feature. They generated a packet length histogram for each webpage. They then captured packet length patterns which were compared with a previously stored pattern. With their classifier that is based on Jaccard's coefficient, they were able to correctly identify 75 % of the sites from their test data, at the cost of a false positive rate of 1.5 %. This is similar to the previous paper [21]. Thus, the same shortcomings apply for this research as well.

Machine Learning (ML) techniques are known to be more robust due to their generalizing ability. The above papers were not using state of the art Machine Learning algorithms. Besides, researchers of the above papers were trying to unveil the websites, not the web-task, which is required to develop ultra-slices. Thus, ML related algorithms were studied as explained below.

A Principle Component Analysis (PCA), K-means and DBSCAN algorithms based DPI algorithm was introduced by Garcia [17]. The research was focused only on video website traffic on cellular networks. The researcher considered YouTube, Flash video over HTTP, Netflix, HTTP Media streaming and Newcamd data flow patterns. 21 features such as the number of packets, mean packet size, maximum packet size, etc… were used to identify the data flow. Then PCA was applied to reduce input feature dimensions. Next, a K-means clustering algorithm with Euclidean distance was used to differentiate traffic patterns. Then results were compared with DBSCAN classifier. The author found K-means to be accurate when it comes to classifying. But DBSCAN was able to identify non-video traffic within the video data flow. Only video data was analysed by the researcher. Additionally, researcher did not considered wireless networks for the experiment and also similar video websites that might have similar fingerprints, for example, YouTube videos and Facebook videos.

Stöber et al. [23] have considered background data activity traffic patterns to fingerprint the web-tasks. Only smartphones data is considered for the experiments. The researchers captured bursts of mobile application traffic (they did not consider video websites in this case) such as Facebook, WhatsApp, Skype, Dropbox, etc…and they extracted a long list of features such as Median absolute deviation (MAD) packet size, quantile packet size, Standard deviation of packet sizes, etc.. They then classified data with the help of a Support Vector Classifier (SVC) and K-Nearest Neighbours. The results show that using approximately 15 minutes of traffic testing (based on 6 hours of training) leads to accuracy of 90% or higher in some situations. Mobile phones use a wireless connection to connect to the internet; hence, the ability of the algorithm to classify Ethernet connections is unknown. The researchers used a single device to capture data thus, the effect of the operating system and the traffic pattern generated by different devices have been neglected.

Wang et al. [24] developed a traffic classifier for encrypted 802.11 WLAN traffic. The researchers have targeted mobile devices such as smartphones and tablets. The authors used various websites to test their algorithm. They used features such as Average size (low 20%) of sent packets, Average size (mid 60%) of sent packets, Average size (high 20%) of sent packets, etc.... They then used a Random Forest (RF) classifier to label the traffic. The classifier was able to recognize applications with about 85% of accuracy. The authors of this research considered two different wireless networks from two different locations. The authors did not consider similar applications thus misclassification for similar applications such as WhatsApp voice calling and Skype voice calling might occur due to similar data patterns. Since wireless connections are different from Ethernet connections the accuracy of classification might drop if one tries to run the algorithm on Ethernet connections.

Aceto et al. [25] suggested a Multi-Classification approach to develop a traffic classifier. They considered packet lengths with a sign indicating direction, minimum packet lengths, maximum packet lengths, median, etc... as their main features to identify about 50 different web applications. They collected data from both Android and Apple devices. The authors discuss various classification algorithms such as Jaccard similarity index, Naïve Bayes (NB), Multinomial NB (MNB) classifier, etc.... They developed an algorithm to combine the results from each classifier to improve the overall performance of mobile application classifiers. They managed to improve results by +8.1% in some cases. However, running various classification methods is computationally expensive compared to other methods, which have good accuracies. The researchers focused on general web applications therefore have not considered video and audio web applications.

S. Rezaei et. al. [26] have developed an algorithm to identify large number of mobile app traffic. The research was conducted by using a deep learning model. They have considered the first 256 bytes of the header and the payload information of the first 6 packets regardless of the direction. Then a vector of 1536 values was developed simply by concatenating all the bytes. This vector was fed to a deep CNN network to classify the mobile app. Identifying ambiguous flow is one of the main objectives of the research, thus to identify ambiguous flow they have concatenated the relative time for the CNN's result. After concatenating for about 2 seconds they fed, it to an LSTM based RNN to identify the ambiguous flow. Authors have tested the algorithm with 80 different apps and have achieved 84% to 98% accuracy. The research is focused on mobile data and also identifying mobile application is the main goal, which is different from identifying web-tasks. Information about the dataset was not sufficient. It is unclear if the accuracy is for off-line data or otherwise. Researchers have considered the relative time as a feature, thus the performance of the algorithm in a slow network is questionable.

There are numerous papers on traffic classification on the internet however; none of them focuses on developing traffic classification for network slicing. None of the researchers (to our knowledge) has conducted research to identify web-tasks, which is different from identifying websites. Based on the reviewed literature, packet length was used by many researchers as their main feature. Most of the researchers did not consider both Wireless and Ethernet connections at once. However, as the Ethernet connections are faster than wireless connections, it is possible to generate different packet length sizes. According to the above-discussed papers, it is clear that researchers who adopted modern-day technologies such as K-mean, SVM, etc. achieved higher accuracy. This suggests that using recent ML algorithms improves classification results.

2.4 5G Orchestration and Slicing Use Cases

Not many papers have been published in regard to 5G slicing with the help of orchestrator and ML in the networking field. Thus, few useful papers were studied in this area. Although ML algorithms existed in the past, due to a large amount of data produced by consumers, ML has become one of the most robust methods to manage today's internet consumers. Imad et al. [27] have used ML in the data plane to forecast User Equipment (UE) requests for the 5G Core Access and Mobility Management Function (AMF) to reduce the percentage of rejection due to request bottleneck. They predict future UE requests by using a Feed-Forward NN with three layers and also by using an RNN. Hence, informing AMF of 5G core beforehand to scale out for the future requirement. This has reduced the drop out amount due to a high number of UE requests. The researchers found the RNN to be the most accurate (90% of accuracy have been achieved with RNN) in this case.

R. Ferrús et. al. [28] propose a framework to slice the RAN by using definition descriptors. The researchers present two main purposes of performing network slicing, namely providing a particular system behaviour and particular tenant. The authors explain that a slice would be recognized by a unique Slice_ID by the 5G Core network. Then based on the ID, the 5G Core would allocate functionalities for control plane and for the user plane of the slice. They have identified three main issues that need attention when slicing within a cell and propose to split the RF carrier resources for a period of time with a specific frequency. This research is focusing on allocation and identification at the radio level, which is different from this book. However, this paper shows that slicing will be applied to a device or for a set of devices based on RAN_Slicing_ID.

Politis et. al. [29] showcases how can a 5G network could be deployed anywhere in the world by using a satellite connection as the backhaul network. They have attached a satellite to a vehicle with 5G Edge Node in the vehicle. They then integrated the 5G Core to SatCore. Thus the SatRAN acts like a 5G RAN whereas the vehicle acts as the user equipment for the 5G Network. The system explained in the paper is capable of deploying eMBB and mMTC slices in a rural area or in an emergency within minutes.

Corici et. al. [30] Proposes an ML-based fault detection to overcome the performance decaying in 5G Network due to softwarization. Due to the deployment of virtual networks in parallel to each other, it is required to monitor the status of the network and adapt accordingly. Thus, authors of this paper propose an anomaly detection by using LSTM cells. The result was then converted to network policies and then fed to NFV environment to take necessary actions. The researchers have used Open 5G Core as their NFV environment, and they have managed to detect more anomalies than the regular NFM fault detection system within 100 ms.

Ramon et al. [31] have proposed an architecture to enable ML to develop in the multilayer transport networks. In this paper, they discuss taking advantage of 5G technologies such as Software Defined Networking (SDN) to manage metropolitan networks which is actually a use case of 5G technology.

Ved et al. [32] proposed ML for slicing. The authors discussed the automation of network functions related to network slicing. The paper shows network functions and relevant machine learning techniques which could be used to get the best results. However, the author have not applied ML to solve issues.

Akihiro et al. [33] have achieved mobile virtual network operation (MNVO) via SDN. The researchers considered IP data packet header information and length mean as their features. They have identified mobile applications with 80% accuracy with the random forest algorithm. Then they have modified the IP packet with newly appended data to identify the application during the SDN stage.

In 2017 Akihiro et al. have published another paper [34] examining the characteristics of LTE Radio Access Network (RAN) for device-specific slicing. They have studied the differences between 3G and LTE networks and they have not found any significant difference between 3G and LTE for bandwidth-constrained MNVOs.

According to the above papers, it is clear that ML has been applied in the field of 5G orchestration and slicing to solve various network related issues. However, nobody has tried to use a 5G orchestrator or 5G mobile core to develop slices within eMBB slice, especially based on the web task. Thus, this book presents a unique use case of network slicing.

2.5 Summary of Chapter Two

In this chapter website finger printing research papers were analysed first and next 5G slicing research papers were analysed. Website finger printing was divided into port-based methods, payload-based methods and statistical based methods. Port-based methods alone found to be inefficient in the literature review. Thus researchers have combined port-based methods with other statistical analysis to increase the accuracy. Port-based methods alone are not robust enough to identify Content Distribution Network web-tasks. Hence not suitable for the purpose of this study which led to payload-based methods. According to literature payload-based methods are found to be very accurate. However payload-based methods have low accuracy when predicting encrypted data. In addition it also raises ethical issues which led statistical based methods. Statistical based methods with modern algorithms such as k-means, PCA and ML found to be suitable for this study according to literature. Furthermore Packet length was found to be very common among Statistical based researchers. Next analysed the 5G slicing related papers. ML was applied by many researchers to solve issues in 5G network. But unfortunately failed to find any related research papers in regard to further slicing eMBB based on web-task classification.

3 DATA ANALYSIS

The Exploratory Data Analysis (EDA) method was used to analyse data. EDA is nothing more than understanding data and identifying useful information from it. A set of graphs have been used to understand IP data packets that will be transferred during application communications. Thus, a thorough data analysis is been presented for IP data packets that are captured from varies devices with different settings in this section. It ensures that we are ready to use a Machine Learning (ML) algorithm [35]; it helps to choose the adequate algorithm for the data and it helps to define the most suitable feature variables.

We noticed that there are major differences for the same types tasks on different webpages (as shown on Figure 1-8 and Figure 1-9) thus a unique feature was required to extract web task specific features. Unfortunately, time domain features cannot be used because poor network quality will change the quality of service (for example, YouTube will reduce its video quality) therefore, a different waveform pattern will be generated. After reviewing the literature, it was found that IP packet length would be suitable for the task. Thus, packet length was chosen as the main feature. Packet length is a fixed value therefore at any given time it will transmit a value within the fixed maximum transmission unit (MTU) [36]. Figure 3-1 and Figure 3-2 respectively shows a received packet length histogram and sent packet length histogram of a YouTube video.

Y-axis of the graph shows the packet length frequency and the X-axis of the graph shows the packet length number. Packet length frequency shows how many times the same packet length occur during the captured time period. Since it is a YouTube video, the amount of received packet data should be greater than the sent packet data. This is visible in the Figure 3-1, according to graph user have received about 800 packets, which has a length of 1500 and has sent (Figure 3-2) about 600 packets of a length of 10. Thus the total amount of received packets is about 1200K (800 x 1500) and sent amount is about 6000 (600 x 10). When comparing received amount with sent amount it is clearly understandable that user have received more packets than sent.

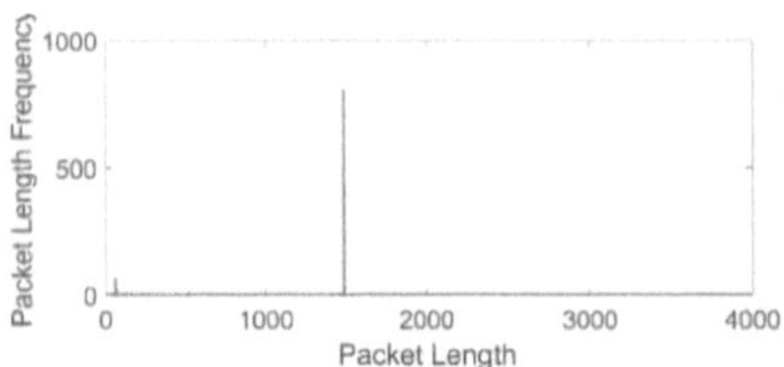

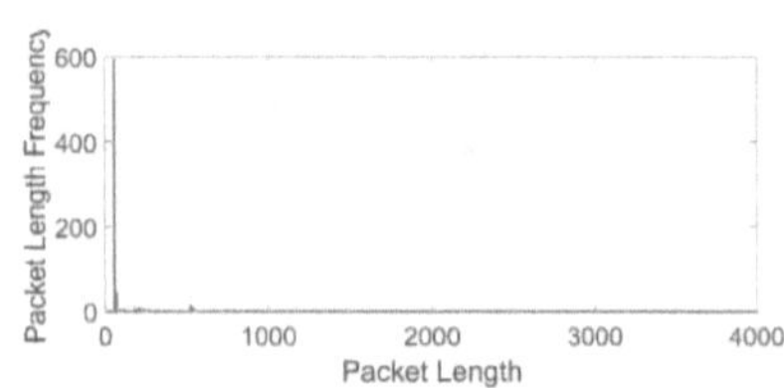

Figure 3-1: Received Packet Length Histogram **Figure 3-2: Sent Packet Length Histogram**

The absolute limitation on TCP IP packet size is 64K (65535 bytes) [37] [36], but in practice, this is far larger than the size of any packet you will see because the lower layers (e.g. Ethernet) have lower packet sizes. The MTU (Maximum Transmission Unit) for Ethernet, for instance, is 1500 bytes. As can be seen in Figure 3-1, there is no activity after packet length 1500. Some types of networks have larger MTUs, and some types have smaller MTUs, but the values are fixed for each physical technology. Notwithstanding 85% of the packet lengths were below 2000 therefore in this work packet lengths higher than 2000 were neglected.

The captured inbound and outbound packet length histograms were converted to a normalized single vector (1D array) to feed this data into an NN, by using the following equation [38], log base 20 was chosen to handle higher bitrates. Therefore, even if a user selects HD video quality, the packet length value would not change dramatically.

$$g_{(r)} = log_{20}\left(l_{(r)}^{v_{(r)}}\right) \tag{3-1}$$

$$k_{(s)} = log_{20}\left(l_{(s)}^{v_{(s)}}\right) \tag{3-2}$$

$$f_{(n)} = g_{(r)} + k_{(r+s)} \tag{3-3}$$

Where,

n: Feature vector index

r: Received packet length number in reverse order

s: Sent packet length number

l: Packet length

v: Frequency of the packet length.

Figure 3-3 shows a normalised graph by using the equation (3-3). On the shown graph, values from 0 to 4000 represent the reversed received (from the web server) packet lengths (filtered by using computer's LAN card MAC address). Hence, 0 to 4000 portion of the figure looks like the horizontal mirror image of Figure 3-1. Due to reversing the feature vector index (X-axis) 0 represents the received packet length of 4000. Similarly, values from 4000 to 8000 represents the sent (from the client's computer) packet lengths from 0 to 4000. Hence, 4000 to 8000 portion of the Figure 3-3 looks similar to the Figure 3-2. Thus, the feature vector index (X-axis) 8000 of Figure 3-3 represents the sent packet length of 4000.

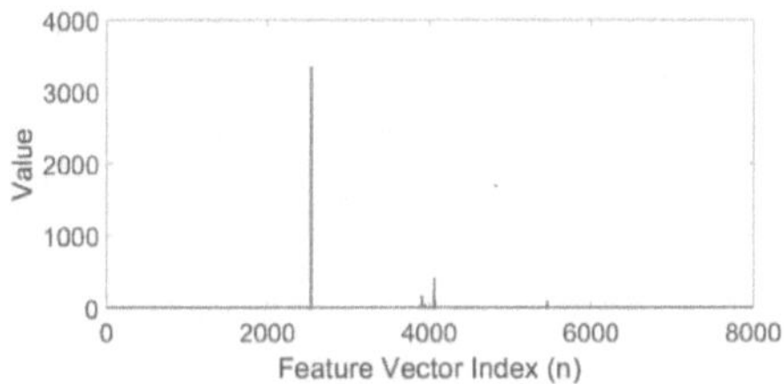

Figure 3-3: Feature Vector f(n) after Equation 3-3

The following Figure 3-4 and Figure 3-5 compare the packet lengths from a Wi-Fi network with the packet lengths from an Ethernet connection. To find out the differences between Wi-Fi and Ethernet watching YouTube in the same network was captured by the same device. In the following graphs, the blue colour line shows the Ethernet connection similarly the brown colour represents the Wi-Fi connection. After feature vector index, 6250 there is no sent packets via Wi-Fi according to Figure 3-5. This means that Wi-Fi have not sent packets lager than 2250 (6250 − 4000 = 2250). When considering 3800 to 4300 (Figure 3-4) it is clear that Wi-Fi has used more packet lengths than Ethernet. Thus, observable proof shows that Ethernet has larger packet lengths compared to Wi-Fi. However, most of the packet lengths are common for both the connections. In these situations, features were extracted by using common packet lengths.

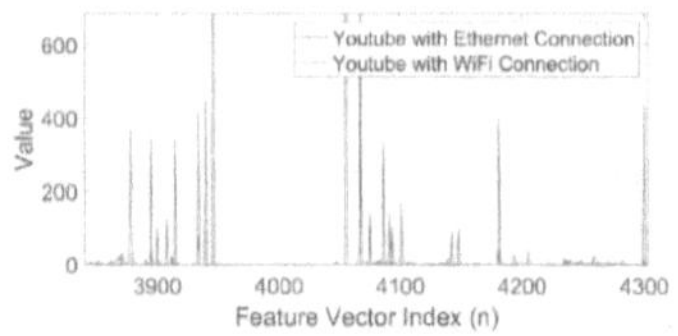

Figure 3-4 : The Area of Small Packet Lengths in the Feature Vector

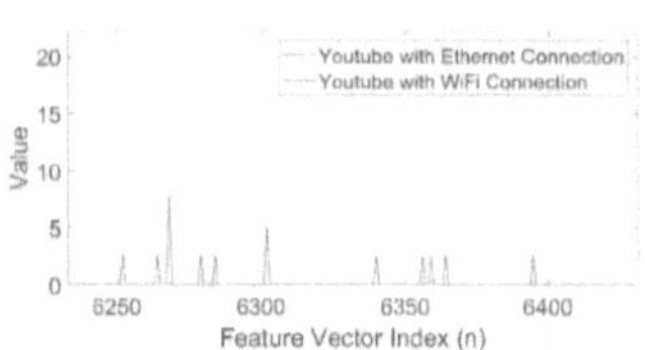

Figure 3-5 : The Area of Sent Lager Packet Lengths in the Feature Vector

To find unique features of web application tasks, 30 samples from each application were captured by running the web application tasks for a minute. However, after about 20 seconds YouTube videos start to play videos from the buffered data, thus 5 seconds of data every 5 seconds (from four different time windows) were extracted for the analysis. Therefore, packets transferred within 5 seconds were used as the raw data. All the other web browsers and other applications that use the internet were closed while sniffing. Recording packets started from the moment it sends the DNS request. Altogether a total of 120 samples were captured from each web-task for the EDA process. Figure 3-6 shows a superimposed graph of all 600 samples data.

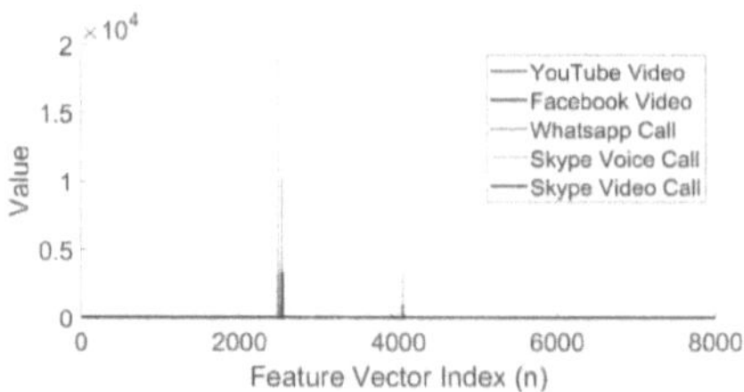

Figure 3-6: All Data Analysis Samples

The blue and red spikes around f(2500) shows that YouTube and Facebook receive lots of data via packet lengths around 1500 (those are the payloads which contains the actual video information) over WhatsApp and Skype. For such dominating values the logarithmic value (equation 3-4) of those points were extracted as features. According to graph in Figure 3-6 the data related Skype and WhatsApp are almost negligible. That also gives an idea about the amount data consumption when watching a video compared to video chatting on Skype in first minute. However, Figure 3-7 shows a magnified graph around f(4100) in the feature vector. It is visible that different application tasks generated different patterns in the feature vector around f(4100).

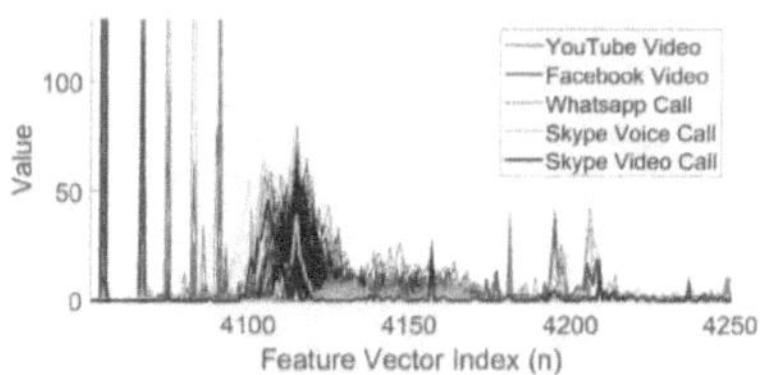

Figure 3-7: Zoomed Data Samples

According to Figure 3-7, YouTube and Facebook use specific packet lengths, and WhatsApp and Skype are using a range of normalized packet lengths. As show on the graph Skype is using smaller packet lengths for voice around f(4115) and WhatsApp is using a range of packet lengths(f(4120) to f(4170)). WhatsApp and Skype distribution of normalized packet lengths looks like a bell in shape. Hence, Standard Deviation (SD), Area (A) and the Base Length (BL) of the bell were chosen to extract as features by using following equations.

For YouTube and Facebook:

$$V = log_x(f_{(n)})\qquad(3\text{-}4)$$

For Skype and WhatsApp:

$$SD = \sqrt{\frac{\sum_{n=ns}^{n=ne}|f(n)-\mu|^2}{N}}\qquad(3\text{-}5)$$

$$A_{ne-ns} = \int_{ns}^{ne} f(n)d_n\qquad(3\text{-}6)$$

$$BL = \sum_{n=ns}^{n=ne} f(n) = \begin{cases} p+1 & if\ f(n) > 0 \\ 0 & Otherwise \end{cases}\qquad(3\text{-}7)$$

Where,

N = ne - ns

ns – Starting feature vector index

ne – Ending feature vector index

n – Feature vector index

x – Base of the logarithmic value (determined based on the feature)

N – Number of data point

µ – Mean of the range (ne - ns)

Feature extraction for each web application tasks is described in the feature extraction section (in Chapter 5 section 5.1.3) under the methodology section.

3.1 Summary of Chapter Three

In this chapter, we examined the captured data to identify key data patterns, features and dependencies. Calculated packet length histogram graphs showed that the packet length used for the same web-task differs with the connection type. Graphs reviled that the packet lengths greater than 2000 were negligible. We observed that both YouTube video and Facebook video have similar data patterns and also WhatsApp and Skype voice calling. Although Skype video calling also sending and receiving video data we noticed that the data pattern generated by Skype video calling is very different from YouTube video and Facebook video. Finally, based on common data patterns four equations were identified to extract features.

4 AI BACKGROUND STUDIES

After reviewing the related literature and completing the data analysis, it is clear that using recent technologies will increase the accuracy of the web-task classifier. In this section, four different ML algorithms were briefly explained for the purpose of understanding the concepts and parameters behind these algorithms. Namely, Support Vector Machines (SVM), Multi-layer Perceptron (MLP), Convolutional Neural Networks (CNN) and Recurrent Neural Network (RNN). These algorithms were used with different parameter settings in the Chapter 5 to find the best classifier.

4.1 Support Vector Machine (SVM)

Support Vector Machines (SVMs) [39] [40] [41] [42] have been used many times since 1998 after Vladimir N. Vapnik first introduced the concept. It is usually applied to pattern classification problems and as well as to solve nonlinear regressions issues. In this book, SVMs were used to recognize IP packet data patterns.

SVM is a discriminative classifier formally defined by a separating hyperplane [39]. In other words, the SVM algorithm is capable of generating an optimal hyperplane for known (labelled) data. Then the generated hyperplane is used by the algorithm to categorize new examples. In two-dimensional space, this hyperplane is a line dividing a plane in two parts where in each class lies on either side.

The logic behind SVM is easy to understand with simple examples. As shown in Figure 4-1 (a) let's consider two separate classes (circles and triangles) which require distinction. The best hyperplane (line) which separates the two is shown in Figure 4-1 (b). However, what makes (Figure 4-1 (b)) the best, because there can be infinite hyperplanes in between given two classes (triangles and circles) SVMs decides the best hyperplane as the hyperplane which has the maximum distance to the closest tag (Figure 4-1 (c)).

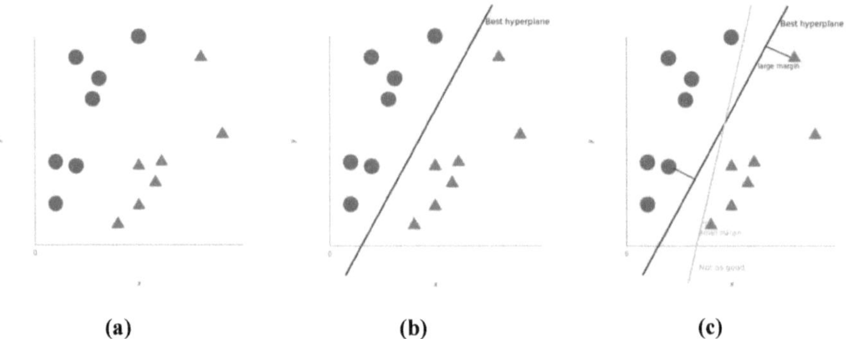

(a)   (b)   (c)

Figure 4-1: Hyperplane of SVM [40]

For non-linear issues SVM considers multi-dimensions and finds the best hyperplane in another dimension as shown in Figure 4-2. It is clear that according to Figure 4-2 (a) two classes cannot be distinguished by a straight line. But if one considers another dimension which is $z = x^2 + y^2$. This will give us a three-dimensional space (x, y and z) where the z plane can be shown as in Figure 4-2 (b). These kind of transformations are called kernels. Now given two classes (triangles and circle) are clearly separable, thus can find the best hyperplane which separate two classes. Finally, if one converts back from z plane to x, y plane the hyperplane would be visible as in Figure 4-2 (c).

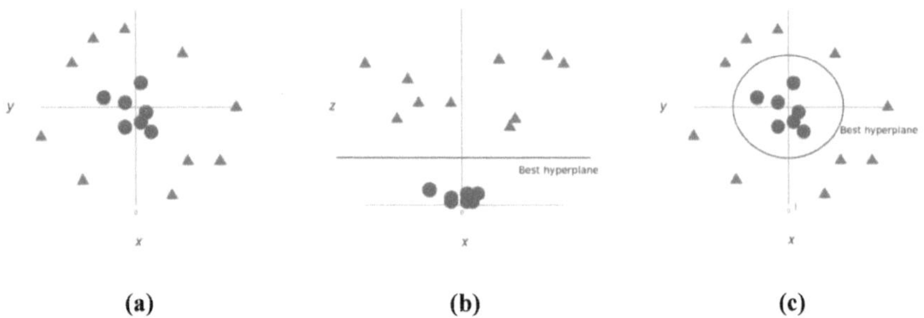

(a)   (b)   (c)

Figure 4-2: Nonlinear SVM Hyperplane [40]

For the above issue, it is clearly visible that a circular dimension z would solve the issue. However considering a dimension for a real-world data set which consists millions of data points may not easy as it seems. There can be many new dimensions, each one of them possibly involving a complicated calculation. However, according to mathematical equations [41] [42], SVM doesn't need the actual vector to determine the best hyperplane. It can get the corresponding new space just by calculating the dot product of new space equation (which is z in the previous example $z = x^2 + y^2$) with the existing dimensional space. This means that we can sidestep the computationally expensive calculations of the new dimensions. Imagine two scalar values of two-dimensional space called "a" and "b".

Imagine the new space we want:

$$z = x^2 + y^2 \qquad\qquad (4\text{-}1)$$

Figure out what the dot product in that space looks like:

$$a.b = x_a.x_b + y_a.y_b + z_a.z_b \qquad\qquad (4\text{-}2)$$

$$a.b = x_a.x_b + y_a.y_b + (x_a^2 + y_a^2).(x_b^2 + y_b^2) \qquad\qquad (4\text{-}3)$$

Now SVM can apply its equations by using the new dot product.

The function used to transform is called a kernel function (z). Most of the time kernel would be a linear function which is used to perform linear classification. Note that the kernel trick is not actually part of SVM. It can be used with other linear classifiers such as logistic regression. An SVM only takes care of finding the decision boundary.

The Regularization parameter (often termed as C parameter) is the misclassifying amount allowed to avoid in each training iteration. The chosen hyperplane would have a smaller class margin for large values of C, if that hyperplane does a better job of getting all the training points classified correctly. Conversely, a very small value of C will cause the optimizer to look for a larger-margin separating hyperplane, even if that hyperplane misclassifies more points. Two figures shown below are depicting the results of two C values. Figure 4-3 (a) shows the misclassification due to lower regularization value. Figure 4-3 (b) shows the result for a higher C value.

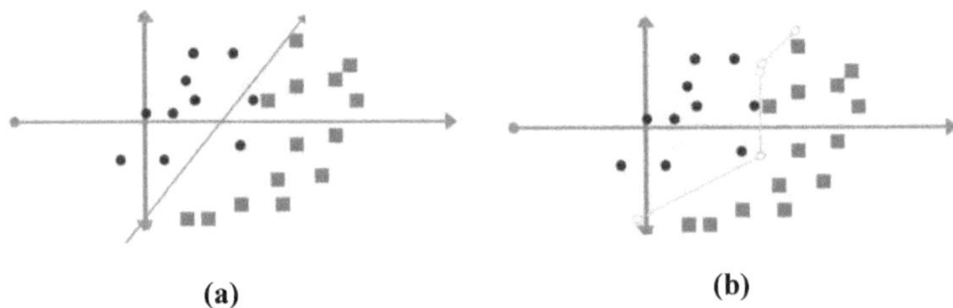

(a)   (b)

Figure 4-3: SVM C Values [39]

To solve nonlinear issues SVM uses exponential kernels (same as z kernel) [41] [42]. One of the common kernel used by SVM has shown below. Where x is the input and x' is the support vectors.

$$K_{(x,x')} = e^{(-\gamma \times \Sigma x - x'^2)} \qquad\qquad (4\text{-}4)\ [39]$$

The variable gamma determines the distance considering by the algorithm, from the hyperplanes to find the best hyperplane. Low gamma (Figure 4-4 (b)) will make the algorithm to consider far data points. Whereas high gamma (Figure 4-4 (a)) means the points close to a plausible line are considered in the calculation. Example Figure 4-4 has given below.

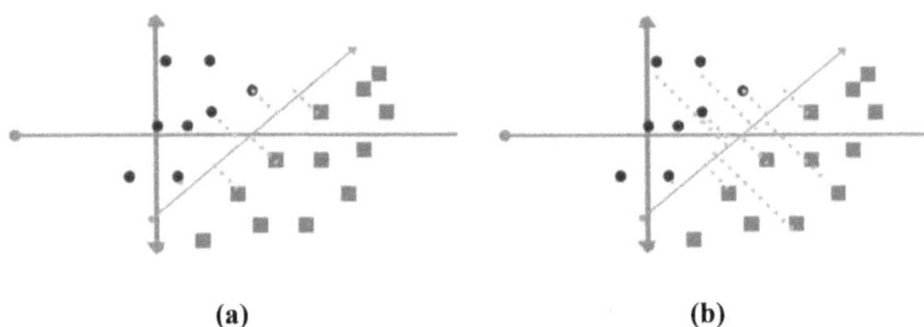

(a)   (b)

Figure 4-4: SVM Gamma Value [39]

4.2 Multi-Layer Perceptron (MLP)

An Artificial Neural Network (ANN) is a mathematical model for information processing. This mathematical model was inspired by the way biological nervous systems (such as the brain) works to process information. The key element of the ANN is the novel ability to arrange bio mimicked mathematical model in various ways to process information systems. These structures are composed of a large number of highly interconnected processing elements (the mathematical models of neurons) which work together for the purpose of solving problems. ANNs learn by using training data same as people learn by experience. ANN's parameters were adjusted for a specific application, such as pattern recognition or data classification, through a learning process. Learning in biological systems involves adjustments to the synaptic connections that exist between the neurons. This is true for ANNs as well [43]. Following Figure 4-5 and Figure 4-6 shows the biological model and the mathematical model (Artificial Neuron (AN)) of the perceptron.

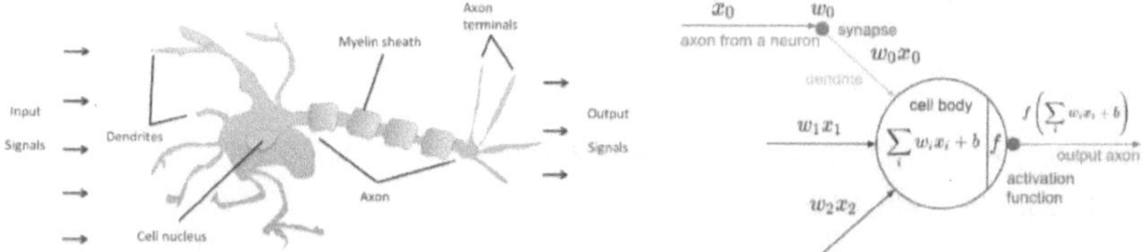

Figure 4-5: Biological Model of Perceptron [44]   **Figure 4-6: Mathematical Model of Perceptron [45]**

As shown in Figure 4-6 all the inputs are multiplied in the dendrite connections and then all the multiplied inputs are added together in the cell body. This value is then applied to an activation function. Bias (b) in Figure 4-6 is the threshold value of activation function. For mathematical convenience, this threshold value was included in the cell body equation.

The most popular neural network model is the Multi-Layer Perceptron (MLP), which is an extension of the single-layer perceptron. Most of the time all the neurons in the previous layer are connected to all the neurons in the next layer. Multi-layer perceptron, in general, are feedforward network, having distinct input, output, and hidden layers. An example architecture (topology) of multi-layered perceptron network is shown in Figure 4-7.

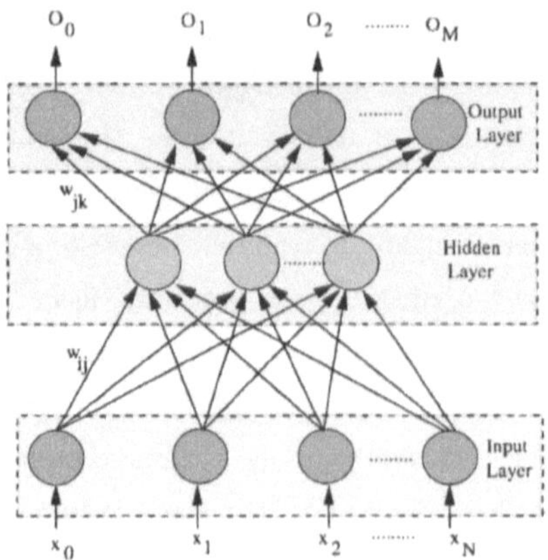

Figure 4-7: Sample Multilayers Perceptron Architecture

Although only one hidden layer is shown in the Figure 4-7 example, MLP-NNs can have multiple hidden layers with multiple neurons in each layer. The neurons of the hidden layer calculate the activation output value and send it to the next layer. Then the next current layer takes those values as their input and computes the activation output. These values are passed to the next layer. This process continues until the output layer, which produces the actual response of the NN to the given input. The process of data passing to the layer in front is called the Feed Forward method. The values generated from the output layer are compared with the desired outputs. Actual output neuron values would deviate from the labelled value (desired) which will result in an error at the output layer. This error is used to compute the error of the layer before the output layer. Similarly, the error of each layer would be used to calculate the error of the layer before till the input layer. This process of propagating error backwards until the input layer was called backpropagation.

The above-mentioned method can be described in mathematics [46] as follows. The net input to the jth neuron (Figure 4-7) can be shown as below:

$$I_j = \sum_{n=1}^{N} x_n \omega_{ij} + \theta_j \tag{4-5}$$

Thus the output of the jth neuron can be shown as:

$$O_j = f_j(I_j) = \frac{1}{1 - e^{(-I_j)}} \tag{4-6}$$

Where $x_1, x_2, \ldots, x_n$ is the input vector, weights w_{ij} represents the weight between the hidden layer and the input layer, and θ_j is the bias term associated with each neurone in the layer.

After applying the above concepts the new weights for the output layer can be calculated as shown below.

$$\omega_{jk}^{(new)} = \omega_{jk}^{(old)} + \eta \delta_j O_j \tag{4-7}$$

Where η is the learning rate of the hidden layer neurons. Similarly, δ can be denoted by,

$$\delta_j = O_j(1 - O_j)(T_j - O_j) \tag{4-8}$$

Where T_j is the expected output or in other words given target value. Following the chain rule, δ_i, for the ith layer can be similarly obtained. The equation for changing the weights between the input and hidden layers can similarly be represented as:

$$\omega_{ji}^{(new)} = \omega_{ji}^{(old)} + \eta_2 \delta_i x_i \tag{4-9}$$

Further details about simplification can be found here [46]. However, with modern-day technologies, all the mathematics have been computerized.

4.3 Convolutional Neural Networks (CNN)

Convolutional Neural Networks (CNN) [47] [45] [48] are quite similar to ordinary NNs because they are made up by the same concept of artificial perceptron that change weights and biases via a training algorithm. CNN calculates the convolution of the input matrix a few times before passing the values to the fully connected layer. CNNs are heavily used in image classification algorithms because it will extract features automatically from images due to the convolution process. In addition, computing convolution before sending it to fully connected layer reduces the number of weights and biases required to predict successfully. Layers of convolutions will convert the input matrix into a vector which contains a set of scores.

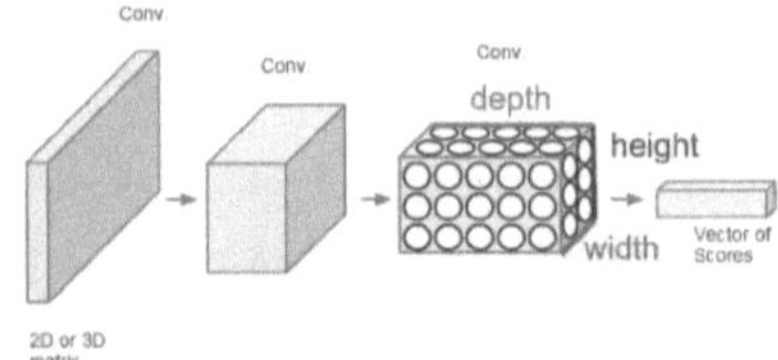

Figure 4-8: CNN's Convolution Process [45]

CNNs does not generate a vector of scores just by convolution process. The basic CNN architecture consists three layers. Namely, Convolution, Pooling Layer and Fully-Connected layer (fully-connected layer is same as MLP). Researchers have stacked them in various ways for different tasks. Some researchers have even introduced transfer functions between layers. Thus there are endless arrangements of architectures [49] for CNNs. However, a basic architecture has been shown down.

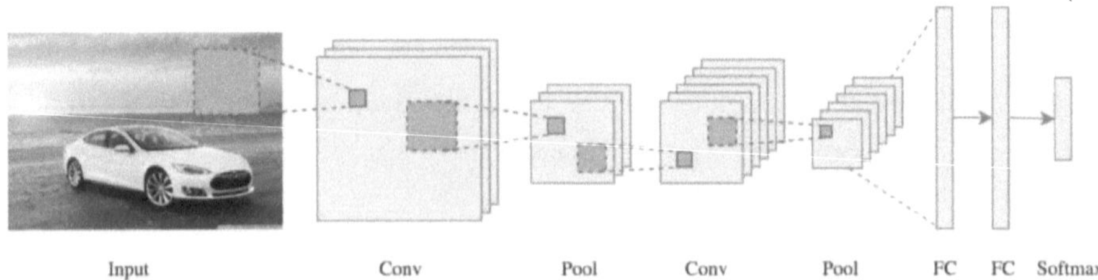

Figure 4-9: CNN Architecture [47]

Although the input vector of this study is 1x50x1 let's consider a 28x28x3 matrix as an example for the explanation.

INPUT: [28x28x3] will hold the raw data points of the feature vector, in this case, a width 28, height 28, and the depth is 3 (in an image this could be three colour channels R, G, B).

CONV layer: Convolution layer will calculate the output values of neurons that are connected to local regions of filter size in the input, each computing a dot product between their weights and a small region (that is equal to kernel size) they are connected to, in the input volume. This may result in volume such as [28x28x12] if we decided to use 12 filters. The kernel size or in other words convolution window size is the matrix that is used to calculate the convolution.

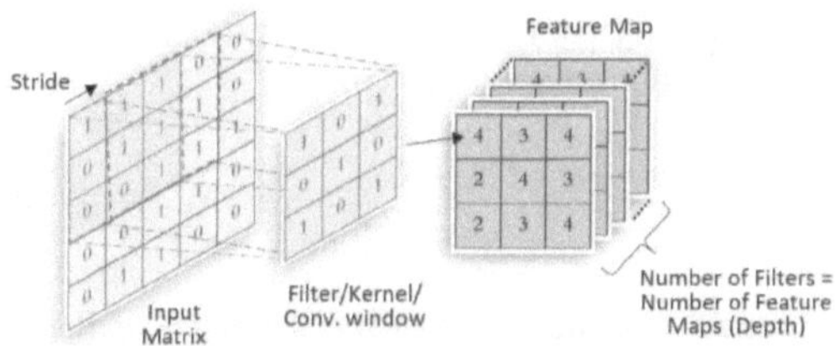

Figure 4-10: CNN's Convolution Window

As it is shown in the Figure 4-10, the convolution (Conv.) window will be a smaller matrix compared to the input matrix. Thus, one needs to move the window to cover the full matrix. The stride specifies how much to move the convolution filter at each step (striding in the polling layer also act as a window shifting function).

RELU layer: This layer is not shown in the Figure 4-10, because usually this layer is included in the Convolution layer. This layer will apply an activation function to each and every element, such as the max(0,x) thresholding at zero. Applying activation will not change the size of convolution output values ([28x28x12]).

POOL layer: the pooling layer usually applies the max operator (gets the maximum value of the pooling window) to down sample the convolution layer output. This step will change the spatial dimensions (width, height), resulting in volume such as [14x14x12]. This enables us to reduce the number of parameters, which both shortens the training time and combats overfitting.

FC layer: the fully connected layer will make the class predictions, resulting in volume of size [1 x 1 x No. Of classes], where each of the output numbers will give a number representing how likely the input is to be in that class. These layers are the same as in MLP where each neuron is connected to every neuron in the next layer.

As shown in Figure 4-9, after many layers CNN converts the input to a final class score. In Tensorflow library, the convolution and fully connected layers calculate the output of each by using activations, weights and biases of the neurons that will be calculated automatically by the training algorithm. However, to use CNNs, some parameters need to be set. As described above windows related to Convolution, stride and pooling. Number of convolution layers and the order of layers need to be found experimentally.

4.4 Recurrent Neural Network (RNN)

Discussed above, NNs consider input matrix given at that moment to make the class decision. But in some cases, it is necessary to know the order of the previous inputs. For example, let's consider the following sentences.

- NN is the best.
- Best the NN is.

If a person needs to find the correct sentence from the above two sentences it is important to remember the previous few words as it goes towards the end. Thus the order of the words defines the correct sentence. Recurrent neural networks were introduced to solve this issue. RNNs have loops within the network which allows for information to persist. To create loops, RNN copies the basic NN architecture multiple times, each network passing the data to the network next to it as shown in Figure 4-11.

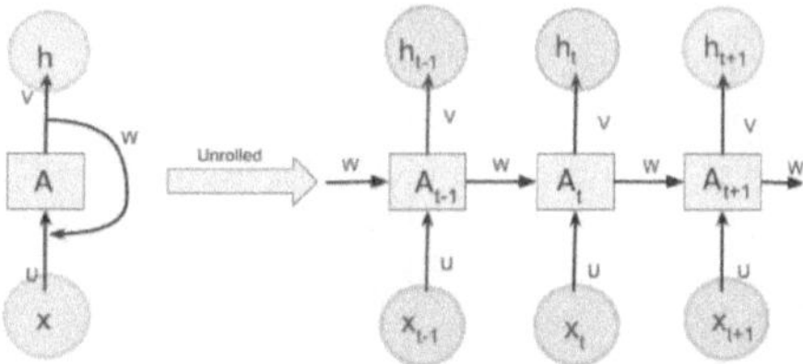

Figure 4-11: LSTM Architecture

Where,

- h_t : The input to the RNN at time t.
- A_t : The state of the A block at time t. A block is a memory block of the RNN.
- O_t : Output generated by each S block at time t.
- U : Weight vector for hidden layer
- V : Weight vector for output layer
- W: Weight vector for different timestamps

U, V and W are common parameters, in other words, time-independent parameters. The significance of this parameter sharing is that RNN model performs the same task at each time step with different input.

The main reasons for the resent success of RNNs are the memory unit in the A block, which is called Long Short-Term Memory (LSTM) cells. Most of the exciting results that have been generated from the RNN networks use LSTM cells. The main objective of LSTM cells is to overcome the long-term dependency issues. Thus, it is capable of remembering a given input for a long period and extract data patterns. Figure 4-12 and Figure 4-13 shows the difference between a standard RNN and an LSTM RNN.

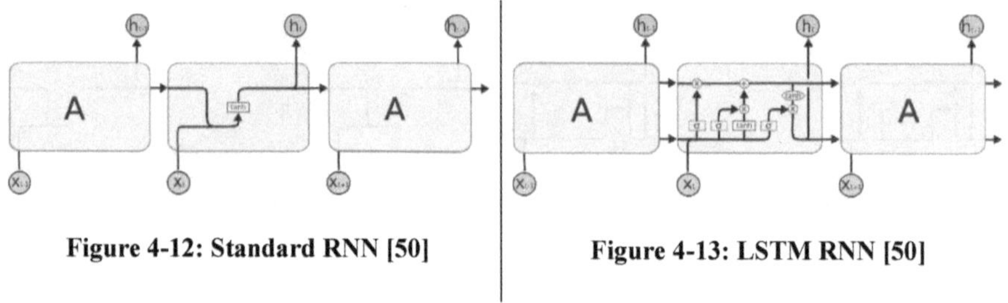

Figure 4-12: Standard RNN [50]　　　　　**Figure 4-13: LSTM RNN [50]**

In standard RNNs, this repeating module will have a very simple structure, such as a single tanh (which is a NN with tanh function) layer. As shown in Figure 4-13 LSTM is handling a bit complicated process compared to normal RNNs. Components of LSTM cell are as follows.

Figure 4-14: LSTM Components [50]

The first step of the LSTM is to decide what information is allowed to follow. This decision was taken based on a sigmoid NN layer called a "forget gate layer". The forget gate layer gets concatenated h_{t-1} and x_t as inputs and outputs a value between 0 and 1. Value 1 means completely keep the C_{t-1} and 0 means don't send C_{t-1} for further calculation.

$$f_t = \sigma\big(W_f \cdot [h_{t-1}, x_t] + b_f\big) \tag{4-10}$$

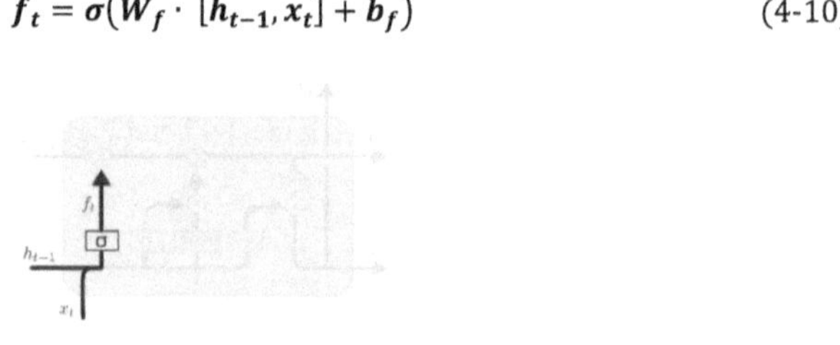

Figure 4-15: LSTM's Forget Gate [50]

Next step is to decide what information should be saved in the current state. Thus a sigma NN called "input gate layer" will decide the values to be updated and next a tanh layer generates a new set of vector ($\hat{C}_t$) that could be added to the current state (shown in Figure 4-16). By combining these two RNN updates the state.

$$i_t = \sigma(W_i \cdot [h_{t-1}, x_t] + b_i) \tag{4-11}$$

$$\hat{C}_t = tanh(W_C \cdot [h_{t-1}, x_t] + b_C) \tag{4-12}$$

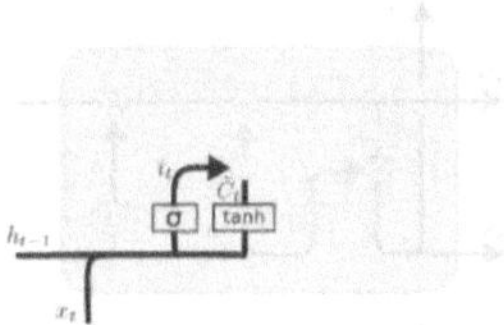

Figure 4-16: LSTM's New State Creation [50]

Updating old cell C_{t-1} to new cell C_t was achieved by multiplying the f_t based on the forget gate layer output and then by adding the multiplication results of i_t and $\hat{C}_t$ as shown in Figure 4-17.

$$C_t = f_t * C_{t-1} + i_t * \hat{C}_t \tag{4-13}$$

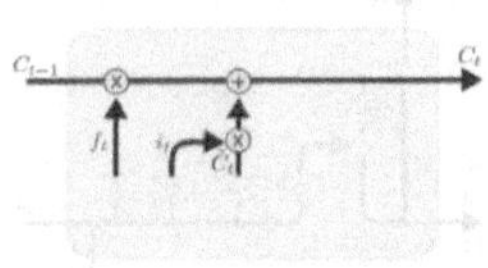

Figure 4-17: LSTM's Cell Updating Process [50]

The decision of output values are made after filtering the present state of the LSTM cell. A sigmoid NN will decide the data that should be output by the cell. Then the present data cell will be sent via a tanh function to normalize values between -1 and +1. Next, the output of tanh is multiplied by the sigmoid NN output values to get the final output of the LSTM cell. This process can be illustrated graphically as in Figure 4-18.

$$o_t = \sigma(W_o \cdot [h_{t-1}, x_t] + b_o) \tag{4-14}$$

$$h_t = o_t * tanh(C_t) \tag{4-15}$$

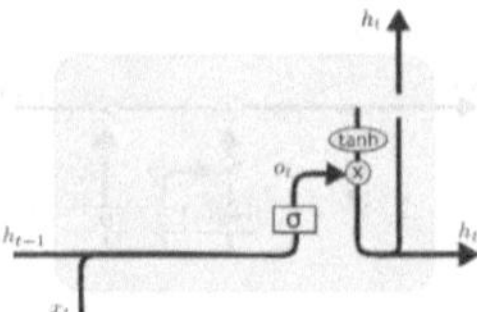

Figure 4-18: LSTM's Final Output [50]

Above discussed is the basic concept of LSTM cell. There are many other arrangements based on the arrangement discussed above [51] [50] [52].

4.5 Summary of Chapter Four

In this chapter, we understood SVM, MLP, CNN and RNN (with LSTM cells) AI algorithms with their hyper-parameters. Under SVM we learned about hyperplanes and kernel trick. In addition the effect of C parameter and gamma which is required to fine-tune the algorithm. Then in the MLP section, the structure of artificial neuron network was explained. Hence studied about input layer, hidden layer and output layer architecture and mathematics behind the topology. Next, the architecture of CNN was explained. In the CNN section we learned about Convolution, Pooling and Fully-Connected layers with concept of window striding. Finally the RNN architecture was explained. Here, we learned the difference between normal RNN and LSTM RNN. In the end section, we learned about the LSTM cell.

5 METHODOLOGY

As shown under Objectives section, there are two main objectives in this study. The first objective is to identify web-tasks, which is discussed in this chapter. The second objective of implementing and using 5G technologies to develop slices is discussed in the next chapter. The first objective of developing a web-task classifier algorithm is discussed in detail in this section.

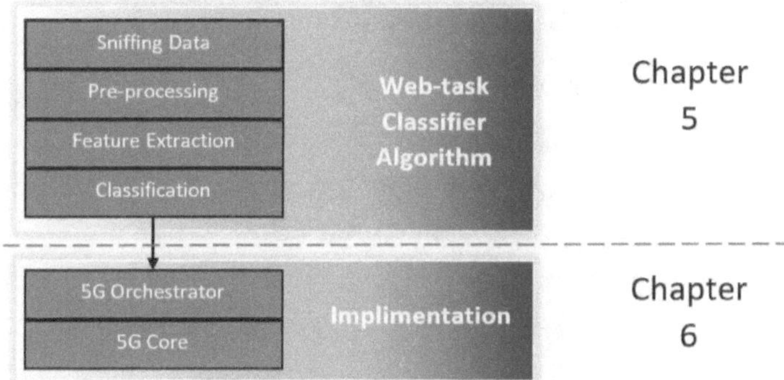

Figure 5-1: Overall Methodology

5.1 Web-task Identification

Web-task identification is similar to website fingerprinting which was studied in the Related Work section. The main difference between a website or web application detector from the web-task detector is the feature selection process. In website detectors, researches have considered data that is unique to websites in the feature extract section. In this book, the author has considered data that is specific to the considered web-tasks.

The approach for the web-task classifier can be divided into three main categories. Namely Pre-processing, Feature Extraction and Classification. The Block diagram of the developed algorithm is illustrated in Figure 5-2.

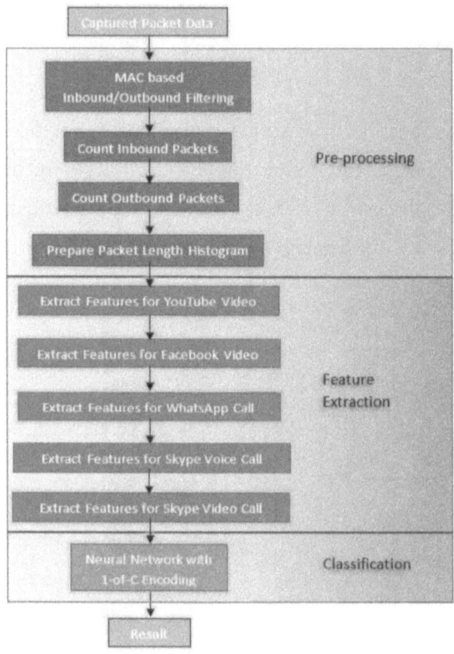

Figure 5-2: Classifier Block Diagram

5.1.1 Captured Packet Data

First, the algorithm finds out active internet connections. If there are two internet connections, it gets the first active connection. Next, it will sniff whatever data packets flowing through it for 5 seconds. Then the captured data is sent to Pre-processing.

5.1.2 Pre-processing

Pre-processing is almost similar to process explained in Chapter 3, but this section shows how exactly the final python algorithm works. As shown in Figure 5-2, pre-processing prepares the data to allow the algorithm to extract features from the data stream. First, the captured data stream was filtered by the active network card's MAC address. The filtered data stream was scanned to find inbound and outbound data. Then inbound data packets were stored to a data array and the same was done to the outbound packets. By looping through arrays, two separate packet length histograms were generated. As described in the Data Analysis section web-tasks do not use all packet lengths. Thus, to make all arrays the same size, zeros were appended for the absent packet lengths. Next, the packet length histogram vector was normalized (by using Equation 3-3).

5.1.3 Feature Extraction

After pre-processing and understanding data, features were extracted from the feature vector for YouTube videos, Facebook videos, WhatsApp voice calls, Skype voice calls and Skype video calls as explained in this section. The equations identified to extract features in the Data Analysis section (Chapter 3) were used in this section. Feature extraction of data will decide the accuracy of the prediction algorithm. If the selected features are not generalized for all the conditions (Ex: Ethernet, Wi-Fi, different video resolutions, etc.), the recognition rate will drop for a new data set. At the same time if the features are too generalized the classifier may misclassify a new data set which is similar to the training data.

Feeding the feature vector generated after equation 3-3 and letting the an ML algorithm to decode features automatically was also tried during the first stage of the research and it generated poor results. The reason is that to differentiate web-tasks, it is required to find web-task specific features and number of features for a web-task are very limited (could be 10, 12, 7, etc.). The probability of finding 10 features from a data array of 8000 is 0.00125. Thus, it is highly unlikely for an ML algorithm to pick those features automatically. Feeding a large data array also takes more time and more computational power, thus only suitable for offline classification.

Features of YouTube videos were extracted first. After plotting all the feature vectors (as explained in the Data Analysis section), visually identified the feature vector indexes which are unique to YouTube video watching. IF ELSE logical filters were used to filter-out the selected features. Let's consider feature 1 which is the feature vector index value of 5435 (f(5435)). As it is clearly visible in the Figure 5-3 none of the other web-tasks using the feature vector index 5435. Thus f(5435) was chosen as a feature for the YouTube videos.

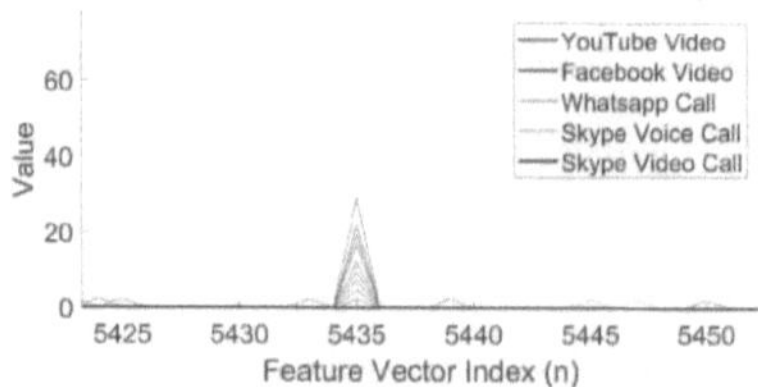

Figure 5-3: YouTube Feature 1

In some situations, a few feature vector index values were added to get a single feature (Feature 2,3,4,6 and 7) as shown in Algorithm 5-1. Let's take feature 2 in Algorithm 5-1, for instance, as visible in following graph (Figure 5-4) some data samples that are active on f(3522), f(3523) and f(3524) are not active on f(3517). We observed that, after about 15 Seconds some of the YouTube videos will start to play from the buffered data. This could be the reason why some data samples are not active compared to other data samples on YouTube. Thus added all the values to create a single feature. Threshold values of the features were derived according to feature vector graph's values axis.

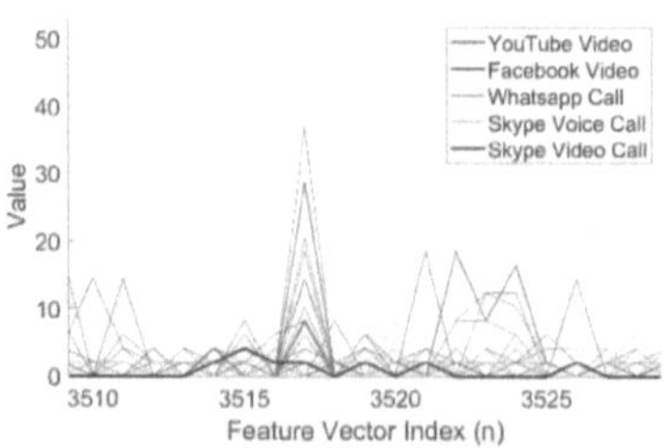

Figure 5-4: YouTube Feature 2

Unlike in Feature 1, feature vector index 4101 of Feature 5 (Figure 5-5) was used by some of the Skype video and voice calls. Nevertheless, adjacent feature indexes were not used by YouTube. Thus because of the data pattern feature vector index 4101 adjacent values were considered to differentiate YouTube videos from others.

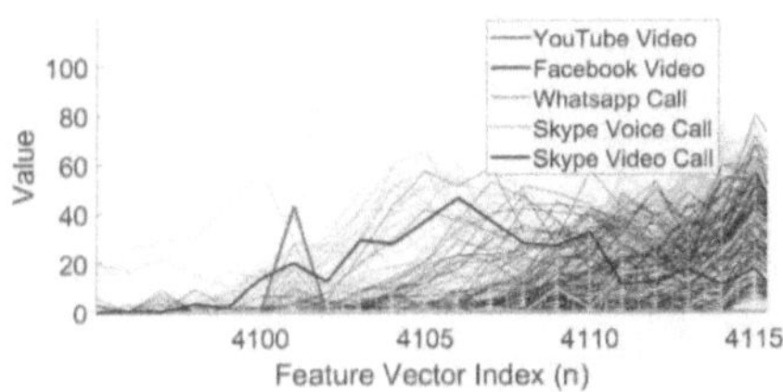

Figure 5-5: YouTube Feature 5

If one notices the logarithmic base values of Feature 6 and Feature 7 in Algorithm 5-1. It is clear that logarithmic base values are different from feature to feature. The base was decided based on the feature vector value axis, a high logarithmic base was used to features that have large values. After considering all the situations seven features were extracted from the feature vector as shown in Algorithm 5-1.

```
1: input f_n                                              ▷ Feature vector graph
2: if f_5435 ≥ 0 then                                     ▷ Feature 1
3:      N_1 ← f_5435
4: if f_3522 + f_3523 + f_3524 + f_3517 ≥ 2.1 then        ▷ Feature 2
5:      N_2 ← f_3522 + f_3523 + f_3524 + f_3517
6: if f_2850 + f_2851 + f_2852 + f_4572 ≥ 0 then          ▷ Feature 3
7:      N_3 ← f_2850 + f_2851 + f_2852 + f_4572
8: if f_2514 + f_2515 + f_2516 + f_2517 + f_2518 ≥ 1 then ▷ Feature 4
9:      N_4 ← log_5(f_2514 + f_2515 + f_2516 + f_2517 + f_2518)
10: if f_4101 ≥ (f_4102 + f_4100)/2 then                  ▷ Feature 5
11:     N_4 ← f_4101
12: if f_3662 + f_3663 + f_3664 ≥ 3 then                  ▷ Feature 6
13:     N_5 ← log_5(f_3662 + f_3663 + f_3664)
14: if f_2486 + f_2494 ≥ 3 then                           ▷ Feature 7
15:     N_6 ← log_10(f_2486 + f_2494)
16: return N_n                                            ▷ Extracted features
```

Algorithm 5-1: YouTube Features Algorithm

Secondly, features of Facebook were extracted. Feature extraction of Facebook video is not that different from feature extraction process of YouTube except for the Feature 5 in Algorithm 5-2. According to following graph, it is clear that Facebook videos are dominating from 4193 to 4203. Thus in Feature 5 the area of the feature vector index from 4193 to 4203 was calculated.

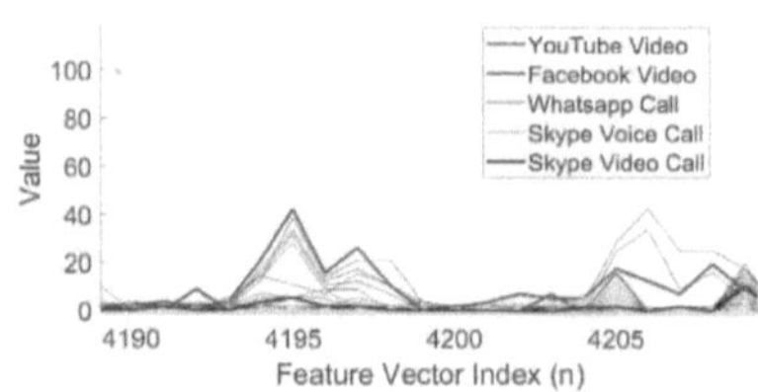

Figure 5-6: Facebook Feature 5

In total six features were identified for Facebook as shown in the Algorithm 5-2.

1: **input** f_n	▷ Feature vector graph
2: **if** $f_{3903} \geq 5$ **then**	
3: $\quad N_1 \leftarrow log_{10}(f_{3903})$	▷ Feature 1
4: **if** $f_{2847} \geq 0$ **then**	
5: $\quad N_2 \leftarrow log_5(f_{2847})$	▷ Feature 2
6: **if** $f_{2626} \geq 0$ **then**	
7: $\quad N_3 \leftarrow log_5(f_{2626})$	▷ Feature 3
8: **if** $f_{2535} \geq 1$ **then**	
9: $\quad N_4 \leftarrow log_{10}(f_{2535})$	▷ Feature 4
10: **if** $area(f_{4193-4203}) \geq 0$ **then**	
11: $\quad N_5 \leftarrow area(f_{4193-4203})/10$	▷ Feature 5
12: **if** $f_{5464} + f_{5494} + f_{5506} \geq 0$ **then**	
13: $\quad N_6 \leftarrow log_{10}(f_{5464} + f_{5494} + f_{5506})$	▷ Feature 6
14: **return** N_n	▷ Extracted features

Algorithm 5-2: Facebook Features Algorithm

Thirdly, WhatsApp calls were considered to extract features. WhatsApp call's feature vector pattern is significantly different from YouTube and Facebook. WhatsApp calls are sending and receiving small data packets in a fixed range as the payload according to data analysis. Feature vector shows that WhatsApp actively receives data in the range of 3780 to 3860. Equations 3-5 and 3-6 were applied to extract features from the mentioned range. The graph below (Figure 5-7) shows the feature vector index range used to extract the first three features for WhatsApp. Not using certain packet lengths (Zeros of the following graphs) also can be used as conditions to generate features. Thus f(4194) + f(4196) + f(4205) having less values and f(3861) + f(3859) = 0 were considered as conditions. In the following algorithm (Algorithm 5-3) "x" represents the number of positive values greater than two for the range of 3780 to 3860 in the feature vector. SD is the standard deviation (Equation 3-5). "area" represents applying Equation 3-6.

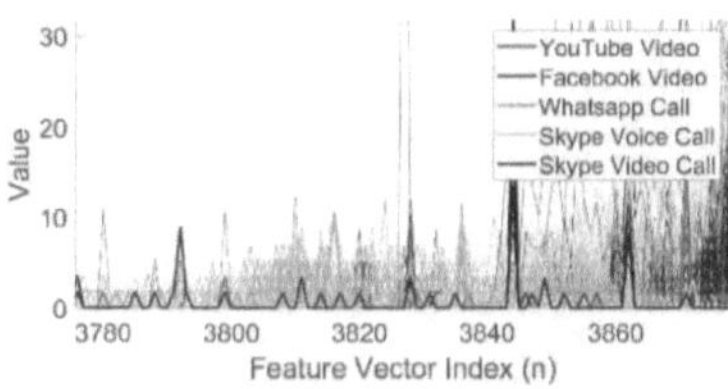

Figure 5-7: WhatsApp Feature 1, 2, 3

Other features are the same as previously explained feature extraction methods except Feature 10, 11 and 12. "Y" represents the number of positive values greater than two for the range of 4109 to 4177 in the feature vector and the "PeakInedx" gives the feature vector index of the peak value for the given range. The "PeakIndex" was used as a condition because the peak value of WhatsApp always at the right side to the 4119 index value which is visible in the Figure 5-8 graph.

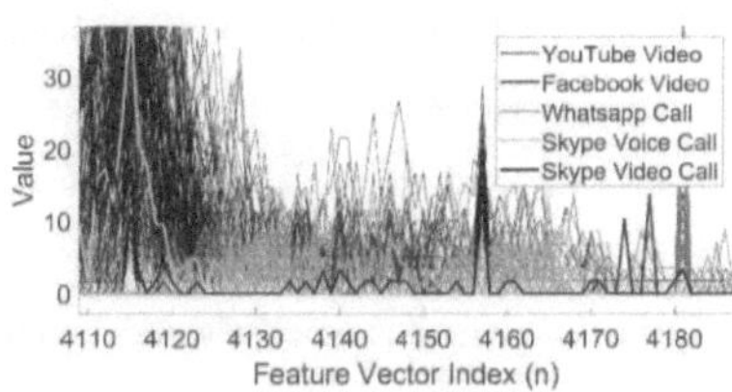

Figure 5-8: WhatsApp Feature 10, 11, 12

Twelve features were extracted in total to separate WhatsApp voice calls from the rest. Feature extraction algorithm for WhatsApp was shown in Algorithm 5-3.

```
 1:  input $f_n$                                                                              ▷ Feature vector graph
 2:  if $x \geq 4$ and $f_{4194} + f_{4196} + f_{4205} \geq 10$ and $f_{3861} + f_{3859} = 0$ then
 3:       $N_{1,2,3} \leftarrow x, SD(f_{3861-3859}), area(f_{3861-3859})$                    ▷ Feature 1,2,3
 4:  if $f_{3835} > 0$ then
 5:       $N_4 \leftarrow f_{3835}$                                                            ▷ Feature 4
 6:  if $f_{4164} \geq 4$ then
 7:       $N_5 \leftarrow f_{4164} + f_{4136}$                                                 ▷ Feature 5
 8:  if $f_{4068} + f_{4069} + f_{4070} > 0$ then
 9:       $N_6 \leftarrow f_{4068} + f_{4069} + f_{4070}$                                      ▷ Feature 6
10:  if $f_{4042} + f_{4048} > 0$ then
11:       $N_7 \leftarrow f_{4042} + f_{4048}$                                                 ▷ Feature 7
12:  if $f_{3955} + f_{3957} > 0$ then
13:       $N_8 \leftarrow f_{3955} + f_{3957}$                                                 ▷ Feature 8
14:  if $f_{3931} + f_{3929} + f_{4070} > 5$ then
15:       $N_9 \leftarrow f_{3931} + f_{3929} + f_{3927}$                                      ▷ Feature 9
16:  if $y > 4$ and $PeakIndex(f_{4079-4159}) > f_{4119}$ and $f_{2535} + f_{4114} = 0$ then
17:       $N_{10,11,12} \leftarrow y, SD(f_{4079-4159}), area(f_{4079-4159})$                 ▷ Feature 10,11,12
18:  return $N_n$                                                                             ▷ Extracted features
```

Algorithm 5-3: WhatsApp Features Algorithm

The fingerprints left by Skype Voice Calls are different from WhatsApp voice calls. However, feature vector index patterns of both the web-tasks are quite similar. This shows that similar web applications are highly likely to generate similar data pattern in the feature vector. However, Skype voice call's data pattern is more concentrated when comparing with WhatsApp voice calls (Figure 5-9 and Figure 5-10). Skype voice calls generates a bell-shaped data pattern thus equation 3-5, 3-6, 3-7 were applied to extract features for Skype voice calls. Features extracted for Skype voice calls are shown in the following Algorithm 5-4.

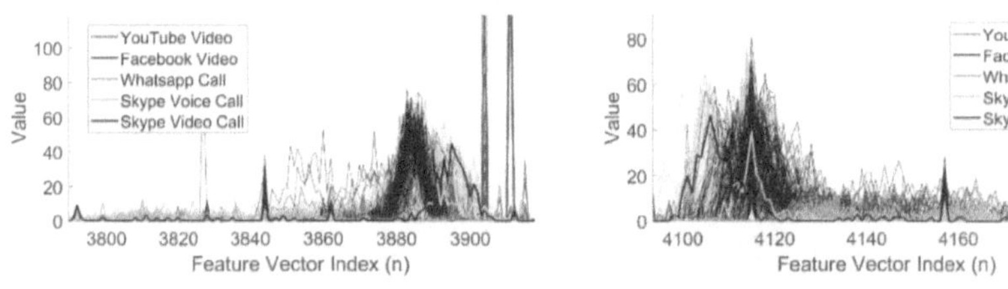

Figure 5-9: Skype Call Feature 4, 5, 6   **Figure 5-10: Skype Call Feature 1, 2, 3**

Comparing to previous algorithms, two new methods have been used in the following Algorithm 5-4 based on the data patterns shown in the above graphs (Figure 5-9 and Figure 5-10). Namely

BL and "PeakValue". BL represents the base length (Equation 3-7) of the bell-shaped data pattern generated by Skype voice calls in the above graphs (Figure 5-9 and Figure 5-10) and "PeakValue" gives the peak value of bell shaped feature vector index pattern generated by Skype voice calls.

```
1:  input f_n                                                        ▷ Feature vector graph
2:  if BL(f_{4090-4150}) ≥ 6 and PeakValue (f_{4090-4150}) ≥ 14 then
3:      N_{1,2,3} ← BL(f_{4090-4150}), SD(f_{4080-4160}), log10(area(f_{4080-4160}))    ▷ Feature 1,2,3
4:  if BL(f_{3837-3910}) ≥ 8 and 15 < PeakValue (f_{3837-3910}) > 85 then
5:      N_{4,5,6} ← BL(f_{3837-3910}), SD(f_{3837-3910}), log10(area(f_{3837-3910}))    ▷ Feature 4,5,6
6:  if f_{3861} > 0 then
7:      N_7 ← f_{3861}                                              ▷ Feature 7
8:  if f_{3885} > 0 then
9:      N_8 ← f_{3885}                                              ▷ Feature 8
10: if f_{4114} > 1 then
11:     N_9 ← log5(f_{4114})                                        ▷ Feature 9
12: if f_{3888} + f_{3861} + f_{3859} > 15 then
13:     N_10 ← f_{3888} + f_{3861} + f_{3859}                       ▷ Feature 10
14: return N_n                                                      ▷ Extracted features
```

Algorithm 5-4: Skype Voice Call Features Algorithm

After separating Skype voice calls from WhatsApp voice calls, it is required to separate skype voice calls from Skype video calls. As shown in Figure 5-10 and Figure 5-9 both Skype video calling and Skype voice calling are using the same range of feature vector indexes since both the IP data traffic are generated by the same application. However, skype video calls are required to send lots of data due to video data. Hence, Skype video calls are using lots of higher packet lengths which is visible in the feature vector graph as shown in Figure 5-11. A similar usage of feature vector indexes can be seen for the received data as well (Figure 5-12). It is noticeable that more data have been received than sent data due to camera quality. Higher resolution cameras sends more data.

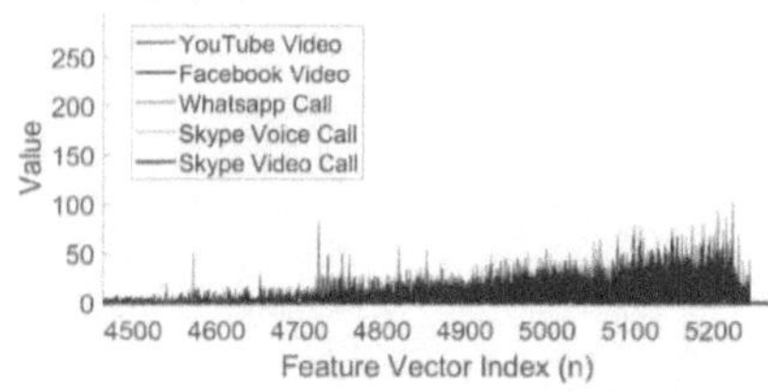

Figure 5-11: Skype Video Sent Data

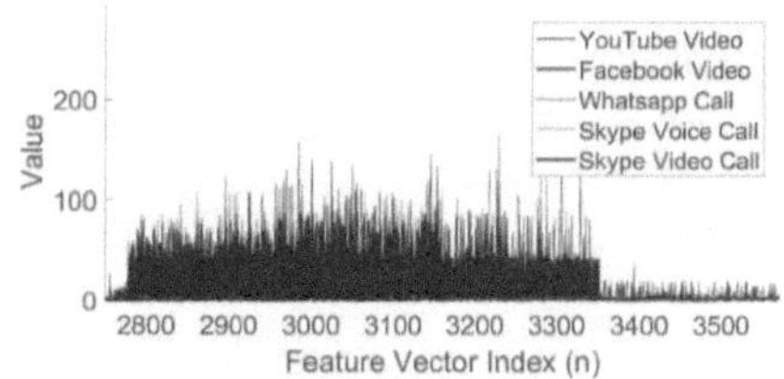

Figure 5-12: Skype Video Received Data

Algorithm 5-5 shows the Skype Video Call feature extraction process. Logical filters used for feature extraction are same as before (No new condition or feature extracting method used). "p", "q", "r", "s" and "t" are the number of values (same as "x" and "y" used in the Algorithm 5-3) higher than a threshold. Threshold values were decided heuristically based on graph data.

1: **input** f_n	▷ Feature vector graph
2: **if** $p \geq 4$ **then**	
3: $\quad N_{1,2,3} \leftarrow p, SD(f_{2800-2962}), log_{10}(area(f_{2800-2962}))$	▷ Feature 1,2,3
4: **if** $q \geq 5$ **then**	
5: $\quad N_{4,5,6} \leftarrow p, SD(f_{2778-2845}), log_{10}(area(f_{2778-2845}))$	▷ Feature 4,5,6
6: **if** $r \geq 4$ **then**	
7: $\quad N_{7,8,9} \leftarrow p, SD(f_{5067-5242}), log_{10}(area(f_{5067-5242}))$	▷ Feature 7,8,9
8: **if** $s \geq 4$ **then**	
9: $\quad N_{10,11,12} \leftarrow p, SD(f_{4841-5067}), log_{10}(area(f_{4841-5067}))$	▷ Feature 10,11,12
10: **if** $t \geq 10$ **then**	
11: $\quad N_{13,14,15} \leftarrow p, SD(f_{3038-3346}), log_{10}(area(f_{3038-3346}))$	▷ Feature 13,14,15
12: **return** N_n	▷ Extracted features

Algorithm 5-5: Skype Video Call Features Algorithm

By appending all the above features of YouTube video watching, Facebook video watching, WhatsApp voice calling, Skype voice calling and Skype video calling a 1x50 vector (N(n) where n=1,2,3…,50) was created for the ML algorithm.

5.1.4 Classification

When analysing the data, it is clear that the same packet lengths from the same task have different values. Following image shows that 4205 index has many Red lines which means that a different number of IP packets have sent by YouTube in each time-period. Thus, many values can be expected for the same feature vector index. Therefore, a generalizing algorithm was required for the classification process.

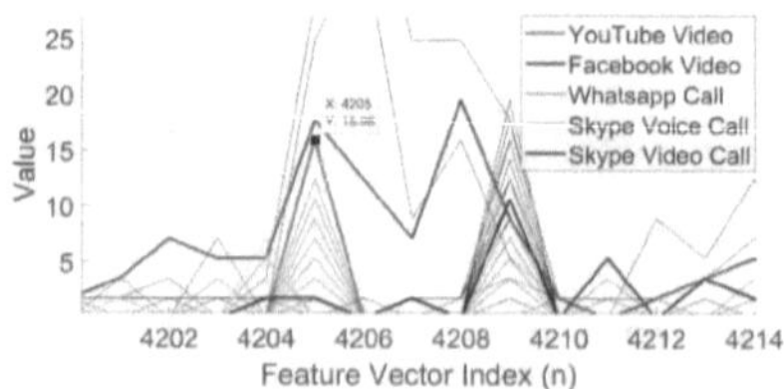

Figure 5-13: Same Feature Different Values

Most of all, predictive nature is required due to missing features. Since all the data patterns for the same web-tasks are not the same, it is not guaranteed that all the features extracted will have a value in every situation. Some of the features will not appear after some time, for example when a person watching YouTube video after about 30 seconds all the video data will be loaded to the RAM. Thus, some features will not appear after 30 seconds. According to studied related work, in these kind of situations ML algorithms have given higher accuracy due to its predictive ability. Hence, two different types of supervised ML algorithms were considered to find the best fit for the live algorithm. These are namely SVM and Neural Networks (NN). NN have been used to develop different types of models as studied in the Chapter 4. Therefore, different ANN models such as MLP, CNN and RNN with different topologies were used to find the best ANN model. Finally, best model was chosen for the live algorithm based on results. Then chosen best model was used to test the reliability.

5.1.4.1 Support Vector Machine (SVM)

To find the best algorithm variable values for the SVM algorithm each variable was changed within a selected range after getting results of few random values. The Best Misclassifying Rate (C) was found to be 110 after varying from 500 to 50 (few random values out of 500 to 50 were considered to confirm 110 is the best possible value). Then best gamma value was found to be 0.001 after varying from 0.0009 to 0.002 (few values out of the range were considered to confirm). Finally, the best Kernel was found to be the Radial Basis Function (RBF) after considering Linear, Sigmoid and Polynomial. The mathematical equation of RBF kernel used for the experiment is shown below, where x and x' are two input samples and x' in some input space and, σ is called a free parameter. Further information can be found here [53]:

$$K_{(x,x')} = e^{\left(-\frac{|x-x'|^2}{2\sigma^2}\right)} \qquad (5\text{-}1)$$

$|x - x'|^2$ may be recognized as the squared Euclidean distance between the two feature vectors. However, with the best hypo parameters, SVM achieved 94.63% of accuracy.

5.1.4.2   MLP Neural Network (NN)

After considering SVM, MLP was used to classify web-tasks. It is important find the best NN topology to get best performance out of MLPs. Thus in this study, the best architecture was found by changing the number of neurons and the number of layers as described below.

Initially the author started with a feedforward fully connected Neural Network with four layers (50, 100, 50, and 5). Then we reduced the first hidden layer neurons from 100 to 30 and calculated the accuracy; Rectified Linear Unit (ReLU) was used as the transfer function. The minimum number of neurons that produced the best accuracy was 64 for the first hidden layer. For the second hidden layer it was 5, if the number of neurons becomes equal to the next layer that layer was removed. Hence, we deleted the second hidden layer because it is equal to the output layer which is 5. Therefore, we ended up with a 50,64,5 neurons arrangement (shown below). The mentioned topology was able to predict with a 94.5% accuracy. Changing the hidden layer transfer functions from ReLU to Sigmoid increased the accuracy from 94.5% to 95.50%. The minimum point of the loss function was found by using Adam Optimizer.

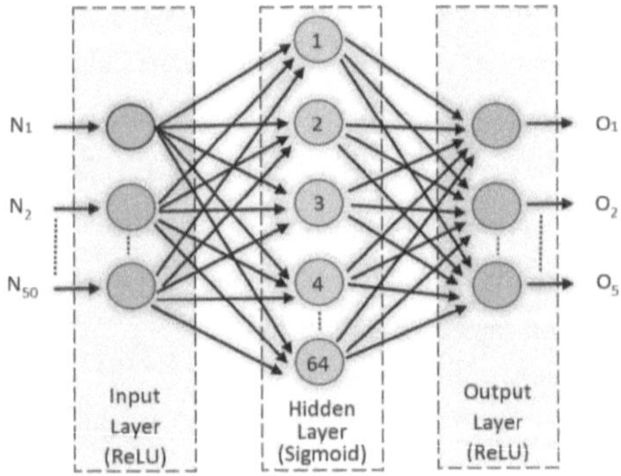

Figure 5-14: Final MLP Architecture

5.1.4.3   Convolutional Neural Networks (CNN)

In this study, a feature vector was already extracted from the raw data. Therefore, CNN is not the best option. However, an experiment was carried out to confirm (the same conditions of MLP were used for the fully connected layers). We started with the convolution, pooling, convolution, pooling, fully connected layer, output layer topology. A 1x5 convolution window with a 1x1 stride was used for the first CNN layer, and a 1x5 convolution window with a 1x4 pooling window with a 1x2 stride was used for the second layer. Next, a fully connected 60 neurons with a 5 neurons output layer was used. This arrangement gave an 84.39% accuracy. When tested without the second convolution layer with 28 fully connected neurons it gave an 85.97% accuracy. It shows that the less the number of convolutional layers, the better the results in this case. Figure 5-15 shows the final architecture of the CNN.

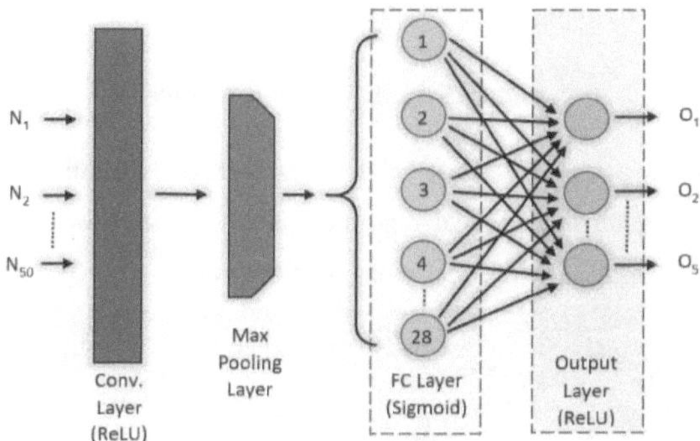

Figure 5-15: CNN Architecture

5.1.4.4   Recurrent Neural Network (RNN)

Generally, RNNs are used for sequence-dependent data. The feature vector sequence of this work is not important. Regardless, we tested by using an input layer, static LSTM, output layer topology RNN network to confirm. The input feature vector was separated into 10 chunks with five values in each chunk and then fed to the LSTM cells. Thus there are 10 LSTM cells in total. Inside the LSTM there are feed-forward NNs as described in the background studies. 70 was found to be the best number of hidden layer neurons in the feed-forward NN of LSTM, after varying from 10 to 90. The minimum point of the loss function was found by using Adam Optimizer. RNN was able to predict with an accuracy of 92.68%. The following Figure 5-16 shows the final RNN architecture. As shown below H_t to H_{t+8} have been neglected since this is a classification.

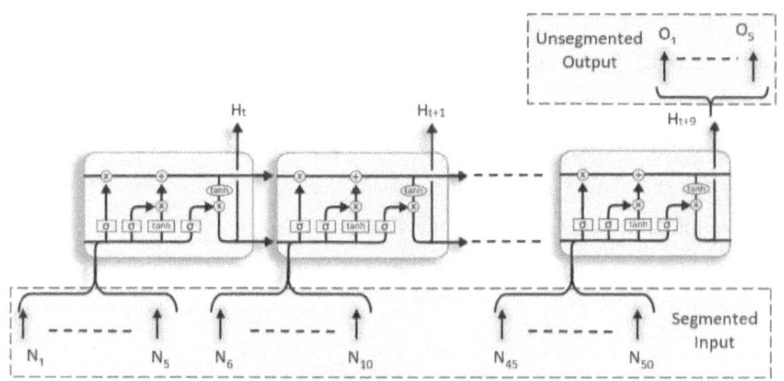

Figure 5-16: RNN Architecture

The Table 5-1 shows the achieved accuracy with the type of AI algorithm. According to the table, MLP is the best option, for this particular problem. Thus the feed-forward MLP NN topology shown in Figure 5-14 was used with backpropagation algorithm.

AI Method	Accuracy (%)
SVM	94.63
MLP	95.50
CNN	85.97
RNN	92.68

Table 5-1: AI Accuracy

5.1.4.5   MLP Training and Fine Tuning

Wireshark was used (just for the initial training set) to capture packets going in and out of the user's PC. Unfortunately, Wireshark is able to capture data only flowing through wires (Ethernet connection, USB tethering, etc.). Therefore, Acrylic Wi-Fi Professional plugins were used to enable Wi-Fi data capturing in Wireshark.

Table 5-2 shows the internet connections that were used for the training data samples with the number of samples. 1-of-C encoding was used to generate targets during the training phase. Therefore, the neuron output of the highest value was used to find the predicted web task.

Web task	Device	Connection Type	Number of Samples
YouTube Video	Laptop	Wi-Fi	40
YouTube Video	Desktop	Ethernet	80
Facebook Video	Laptop	Wi-Fi	120
Skype Voice Call	Desktop	Ethernet	120
Skype Video Call	Desktop	Ethernet	120
WhatsApp Call	Phone	Wi-Fi	120

Table 5-2: Training Samples

A supervised NN allows us to manipulate the training set. In other words, the required NN can be generated by changing the training data. In this work, for the YouTube and Facebook training sets, the last 37 values were set as zeros after calculating the first 13 features. This is done so that the first 13 neurons (in the input layer) of the Neural Network will adapt exclusively for video data. For Skype voice calls, Skype video calls and WhatsApp, the first 13 features were set to zeroes and appended the calculated values for the last 37. Therefore the last 37 neurons of the input layer will adapt exclusively for the Skype and WhatsApp Calls.

Different optimizers were considered to find the best optimizer and to increase reliability. RMSprop, Adam, Momentum, Gradient Descent and Ftrl were considered to find the best.

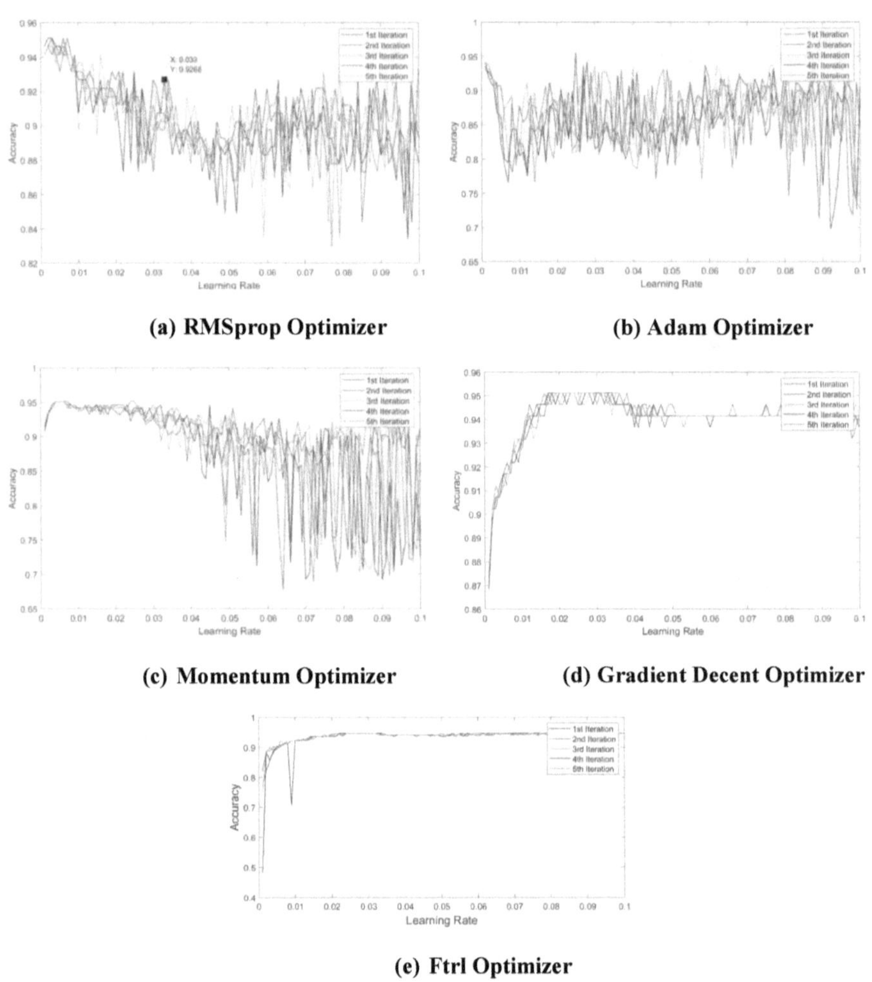

(a) RMSprop Optimizer   **(b) Adam Optimizer**

(c) Momentum Optimizer   **(d) Gradient Decent Optimizer**

(e) Ftrl Optimizer

Figure 5-17: Optimizer Analysis

Figure 5-17 shows the results of tested optimizing algorithms. Above graphs were generated by running optimizing algorithms 5 times to check the reliability of the MLP NN. The learning rate is changed from 0.001 to 1 with the step size of 0.001. According to results, it is clear that

RMSprop, Adam and Momentum are generating vastly different accuracy compared to Gradient Descent and Ftrl. When comparing Gradient Descent and Ftrl, although Ftrl is very reliable, it is visible that Ftrl is generating low accuracy values. Thus, Gradient Descent was chosen as the optimizing algorithm for the MLP NN.

5.2 Summary of Chapter Five

The web-task (YouTube video, Facebook video, WhatsApp voice call, Skype voice call and Skype video call) classifier algorithm was described in this chapter. Thus explained the main steps of the algorithm, which are sniffing, pre-processing, feature extraction and classification. Feature extraction is one of the most discussed sections in this chapter. In the feature extraction section, web-task based features were extracted using the equations identified in the Chapter 3. In total 50 features were extracted to identify sniffed data traffic. Next finding the best classification algorithm was discussed. After fine-tuning hyper-parameters of SVM, MLP, CNN and RNN the most suitable algorithm was selected by comparing the accuracies of each classifier algorithm. MLP became the best classifier with an accuracy of 95.5%. After choosing the best classifier, the training set used for the algorithm and choosing the best optimizer for the algorithm was discussed. After analysing graphs Gradient Descent was selected for the training process. After detecting the web-task, the next main objective is to generate slices based on classification results with the help of a 5G network. This is presented in the next chapter.

6 TESTBED IMPLEMENTATIONS

6.1 Open Baton 5G Slices

6.1.1 Network Function Virtualization (NFV)

NFV, in particular, changed communication networks dramatically which caused the introduction of new management and orchestration functions. These new techniques were introduced to the current model of operations, administration, maintenance and provisioning. Developing a network function was dependent on the network structure in the previous network systems. NFV makes implementing a software function, completely independent from the computation, storage, and networking resources they use. This independence is introducing new challenges of its own such as the Virtualised Network Functions (VNFs), and a new set of relationships between them and the NFV Infrastructure (NFVI). VNFs can be combined with other VNFs and /or Physical Network Functions (PNFs) to make a specific Network Service (NS).

To deploy a network service it is necessary to associated VNFs, VNF Forwarding Graphs (VNFFGs), Virtual Links (VLs), Physical Network Functions (PNFs), NFVI and the relationships between them. These new features of the network require a unique way of management and orchestration. Thus Network Functions Virtualisation Management and Orchestration (NFV-MANO) architectural framework was developed by 5G programmers to manage the NFVI and orchestrate the allocation of resources needed by the NSs and VNFs.

Hence, 5G MANO is responsible for [54]:

1. Management and Orchestration aspects of Network Functions Virtualisation Infrastructure
2. Management and Orchestration aspects of Virtualised Network Functions

3. Management and Orchestration aspects of Network Services

4. Fault and performance management

5. Policy Management

There are only hand full of 5G orchestrators under development in the world [55] [56]. Namely, Open Source MANO (OSM) [57], OPEN-O [58], CORD [59], Gigaspaces Cloudify [60] and Open Baton [61]. Open Baton was introduced by Fraunhofer Fokus research group. This research group also have conducted many types of research in the past, such as its OpenEPC that became a spin-off company named Core Network Dynamics. This group also accustomed to following international standard specifications from groups such as the 3GPP and ETSI. When ETSI published its NFV framework, Fraunhofer quickly recognised a need to work with the MANO aspects. Open Baton was the first research group that started to develop 5G orchestrator, thus have more features and more reliable compared to other 5G orchestrators. Thus, Open Baton 5G orchestrator was chosen as the 5G orchestrator for this study.

6.1.2 Open Baton

The first version of Open Baton was released in 2015 to enable deploying virtual NSs on top of heterogeneous NFV infrastructures. The architecture of Open Baton 5G orchestrator was given below.

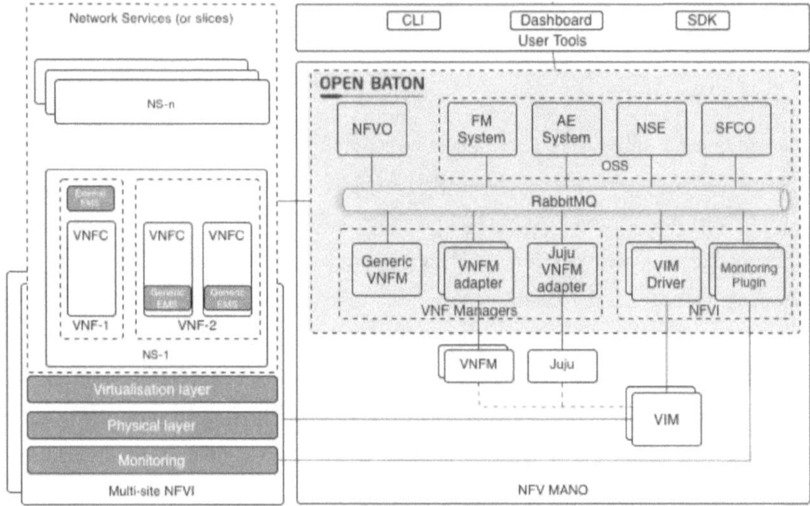

Figure 6-1: Open Baton Architecture [61]

The main components of Open Baton which have been used in the Figure 6-1 are as follow,

- NFVO: Network Function Virtualisation Orchestrator
- VNFM: Generic Virtual Network Function Manager and Generic Element Management System (EMS) able to manage the lifecycle of VNFs based on their descriptors.
- Juju VNFM Adapter: to deploy Juju Charms or Open Baton VNF Packages using the Juju VNFM. A driver mechanism supporting different type of VIMs without having to re-write anything in the orchestration logic.
- VIM driver: A powerful event engine based on a pub/sub mechanism for the dispatching of the lifecycle events execution.
- AE: Auto-scaling Engine is used to automate the runtime management of the scaling operations of your VNFs.
- FM: Fault Management system is used to automatic runtime management of faults which may occur at any level.
- NSE: Network Slicing Engine is used to ensure a specific QoS for your NS.
- Monitoring plugin: integrating Zabbix for monitoring.

In this study, Open Baton was used to generate slices for the detected web-tasks. Thus some modules were not used. Generating slices were achieved as discussed below.

To generate slices Open Baton needs to communicate with Generic VNFM, NFVO, VIM Driver, VIM, Monitoring system and Auto-scaling Engine (AE). The communication between main modules was done via the Massage Queue which is a bus developed by RabbitMQ [62] [63] software. RabbitMQ uses the Advanced Message Queuing Protocol (AMQP) to communicate with Open Batons modules. RabbitMQ is acting as a broker between Open Baton modules thus, solving all software issues (Programming language, version, protocol, etc…). Generic VNFM and NFVO are the key modules of Open Baton these two modules are in charge of deploying the required VNFs. NFVO manages the lifecycle of NSs and interfacing with other VNFMs if required. NFVO reads one or more JSON files which describe the NS (Network Service) called NSD (Network Service Descriptor) and also responsible for the deployment of VNFD (Virtual Network Function Descriptor). NFVO is capable of deploying multiple VNFs (PoPs) as required and it also supports deploying multiple slices in the same Network (Figure 6-2) which is required for this study (slices based on each web-task).

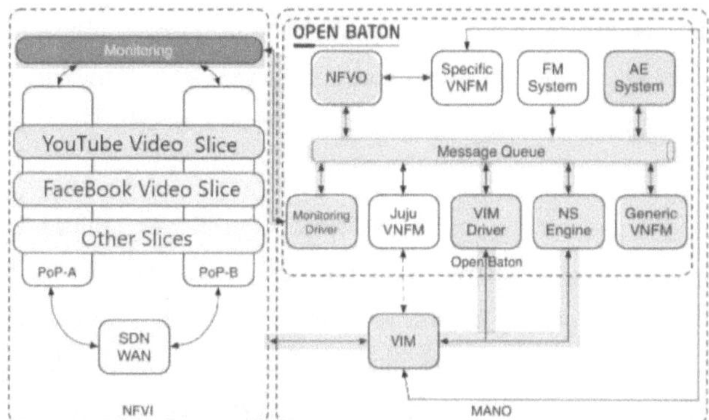

Figure 6-2: Communication Paths of NFVO Deploying NSc and Auto Scaling [61]

Deploying multiple slices was enabled by the Network Slicing Engine (NSE). The NSE instantiates rules on physical networks for allocating dedicated bandwidth as per NS specific requirements. The generic Element Management System (EMS) of Open Baton was in the generic VNFM. Thus, it is responsible for executing the required configuration scripts within the VM instances. Besides, generic VNFM needs to manage the lifecycle of VNFs based on their description.

Open Batons allows to implement different VIMs via its VIM Driver Module. This integration was done via Remote Procedure Call (RPC) [64] mechanism. Thus allows to use an interface that is used by the NFVO. Using of RPC also allows to add or remove different types of VIMs without the need of a modification to the orchestration logic. For this study, OpenStack [65] was integrated with Open Baton via VIM driver.

To know if a requested task was executed or not, Open Baton needs to monitor the tasks that are orchestrated. For this Open Baton has a monitoring driver functional block. In this study, Zabbix [66] plugin was used to monitor information of the VNF components either at the infrastructure level or VNF level. Getting information by integrating Zabbix was done via a monitoring driver that offers an interface compliant with the ETSI NFV specification to communicate directly with Zabbix system.

The key module that has been used in this study is the Auto-scaling Engine System (AES). This module communicates with the monitoring system and NFVO through the massaging bus RabbitMQ to adjust the bandwidth of the slice according to detected web task. This cannot be achieved without fetching the real-time data thus Zabbix and ASE are always communicating to provide automatic runtime management. In addition ASE uses different optimization algorithms to represent the VNFs.

The following setup (Figure 6-3) was used on a testbed for the live experiment. Every 10 seconds (although ML algorithm classifying every 5 seconds it is unnecessary to update bandwidth every 5 seconds) Open Baton checks the classification results of the ML algorithm and based on the result Open Baton's Network Slicing and Auto Scaling engines changes the bandwidth of the virtual switch. Hence gives the best user experience for a particular web task.

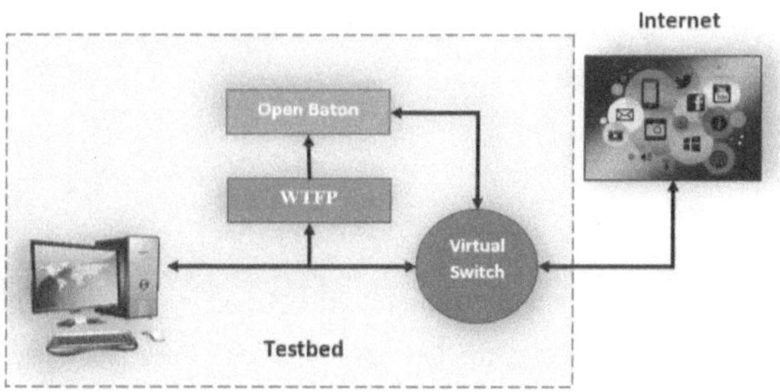

Figure 6-3: Testbed Setup

The table of QoS settings, setup by using Open Baton was given below. These QoS values were assumed to be the best based on the data collected for preliminary studies. Note that the bandwidth given below are for both inbound and outbound traffic.

Web Task	QoS (Bandwidth) in Mbps
YouTube Video	2.00
Facebook Video	5.00
Skype Voice Call	0.15
Skype Video Call	1.00

Table 6-1: QoS Limits

After setting up as described in Table 6-1 experiments were conducted for Skype Video and Skype Voice by using Open Baton as shown in the Results section. However, due to technical difficulties and computer power required, results for Facebook Video, YouTube Video and WhatsApp call were unable to test with the above setup. The refreshing rates of the virtual machine in the OpenStack testbed was devastating when playing videos in the virtual machine which caused the very slow response to mouse movements. Hence made it a very unreliable way to check the algorithm for Facebook Video and YouTube Video web-tasks. Since it is, a virtual machine could not create a hotspot to send WhatsApp traffic via the virtual machine which stopped checking the

WhatsApp calls. These issues hampered further experimenting with Open baton. Thus experiments were continued using Open5G core.

6.2 5G Core

To test our algorithm we used the Open5GCore [67] developed by the Fraunhofer FOKUS. Thus Openbaton acts as the Orchestrator of the Open5G Core. 5G Core architecture with web-task classifier has shown Figure 6-4.

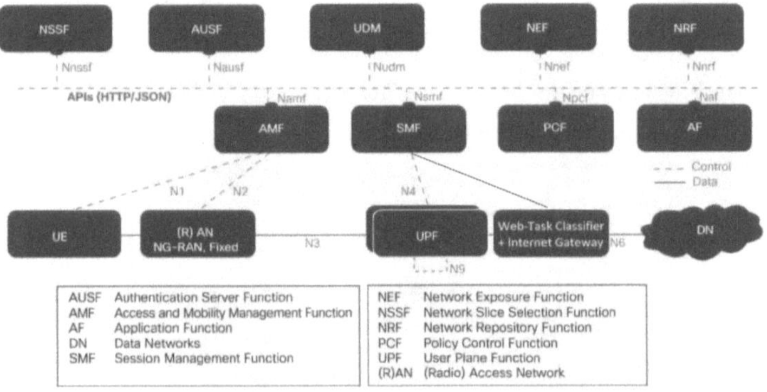

Figure 6-4: 5G Core Architecture [67]

A short description of the main components of 5G core has listed below.

Core Access and Mobility Management Function (AMF): this component is responsible for the access control and mobility. AMF handles the attached requests of UE from several RANs. If the UE is not moving or in other wards fixed access this component is not important.

- Session Management Function (SMF): setting and managing sessions according to the network policy is done by SMF.
- Policy Control Function (PCF): policy framework for network slicing is integrated by this function.

- User Plane Function (UPF): this function is one of the flexible functions of the core. It can be deployed in many configurations based on services and location. It will forward the user's data traffic.
- Unified Data Management (UDM): this component integrates subscriber information for both fixed and mobile access.
- NF Repository Function (NRF): NRF module is responsible for the communication via application programming interface (API) in the core network thus allowing the registration and discovery functionality.

Network slices can be deployed in many ways. If all the components of the Figure 6-4 architecture used for a single slice then it is called a straight forward deployment. Similarly, if some of the functions have shared with many slices it is a shared deployment. In this book, we deploy a straight forward deployment. However, when the devices connected to macro slices suggested in this study are not using the web-tasks that classifier algorithm recognize, it becomes a normal eMBB slice. User data does not flow through control plane modules (AMF, SMF, PCF, AF, NSSF, AUSF, UDM, NEF and NRF). Hence, it flows through RAN, UPFs and internet gateways. Thus for this research web-task classifier algorithm was placed in the internet gateways.

User Plane Function (UPF) is the most important component in this study it is responsible for Packet routing (packet forwarding) and Packet inspection and QoS. Thus after classification, the necessary QoS according to Web task will be communicated to the UPF component of 5G Core. Setting up the relevant QoS (according to 3GPP 5G system architecture) can be shown as illustrated in Figure 6-5. Based on the following architecture it is clear that UPF is capable of processing the marked data and generate protocol data unit (PDU) sessions to the AN to give a specific QoS. Further details about 5G Core can be found here [68].

Another thing to notice in 3GPP 5G system architecture shown in Figure 6-5 is that the user equipment itself is capable to generate QoS flow marking. This is where the suggested system is different from the traditional method. What if this UE is not capable of generating QoS flow marking, in other wards a general device such as a mobile phone with a regular SIM or a home router. Since our web-task classifier is in the internet gateway, it will inform the AN to set the QoS regardless of the device using.

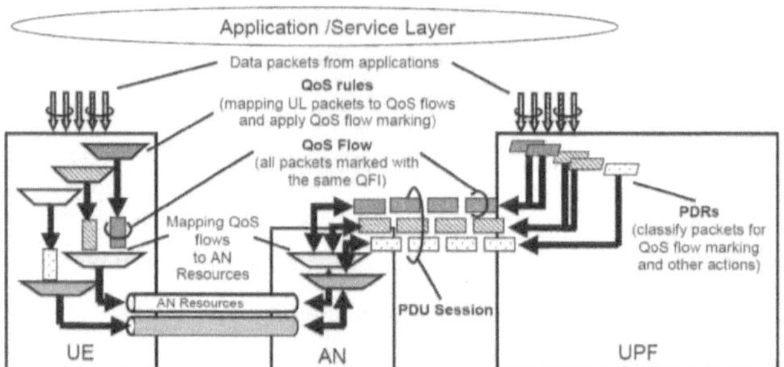

Figure 6-5: UPF and UE Level Classification and Marking for QoS Flows [68]

The Open5G Core was setup on OpenStack to generate QoS based on web-tasks. Here a virtual container was used instead of UE shown in Figure 6-4. Open5G Core did not show any lagging as Open Baton due to the lightweight architecture of Open5G Core. Which helped to conduct experiments hold back by Open Baton (namely Facebook video watching and YouTube video watching). Experiments conducted by Open5G Core have discussed in the Result section. Same QoS table used for Open Baton was used for Open 5G Core as well. However, setting QoS for WhatsApp was unable to test due to lack of equipment in the lab.

6.2.1 Executed commands

First, the 5G Core was started by running the following commands on Linux terminal. All the 5G Core components will run on individual virtual containers.

Figure 6-6: Starting 5G Core

Then "./ph_init.sh" was typed again to bring up the "tmux" session. "tmux" session allows us to access 5G core components (SMF, UPF, AN/enodeB, etc…). The '*' on the bottom shows the present component, the terminal is in. Thus "10: ue_nas*" means that current "tmux" terminal is in ue_nas. "ue_nas" represents the user equipment (UE) of the 5G Core.

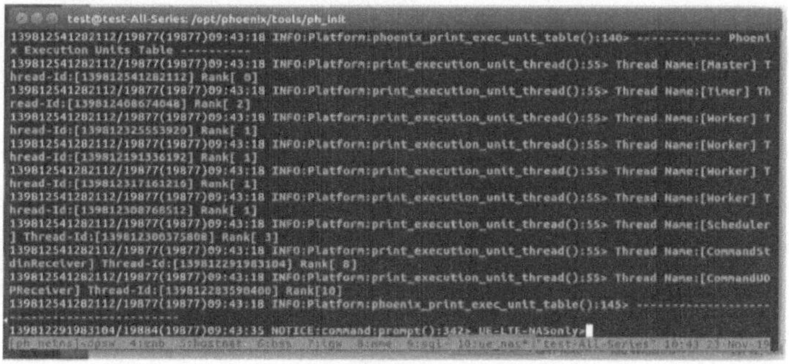

Figure 6-7: Initializing 5G Components

Then "ue.connect_l3 1 LTE-N1" command was executed. This command connects the UE to the 5G Core via enodeB. Then created a new terminal by typing CTRL and B then by typing SHIFT and '. This command will split the terminal into two. Now that we have connected the UE to the 5G Core, UE settings such a browser need to be setup. Thus, UE settings were setup by executing "ip netns exec ue_nas bash".

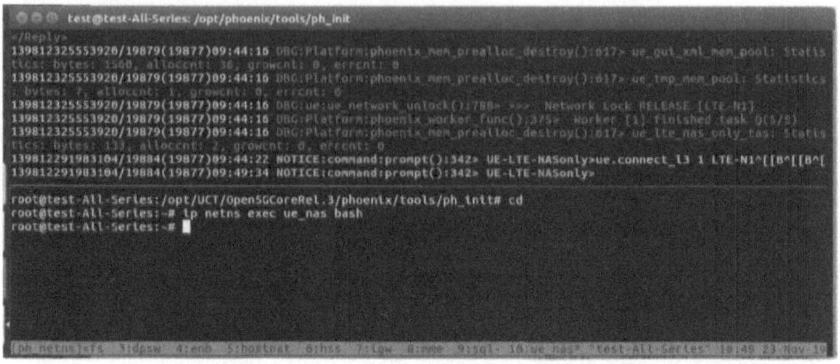

Figure 6-8: Connecting UE to the 5G Core

Then we check the IP of UE by using "ip a" command and next we ping to an Internet server by using "ping www.google.com -c 3" command to check if the internet connection via 5G Core has been established properly. Then we start the user by executing "service ssh start" and next we checked the status by running "service ssh status". Status results have shown down.

Figure 6-9: Verification of Internet Connection via 5G Core

Then we execute "/usr/sbin/sshd -o PidFile=/run/sshd.pid" command to set final settings. ".pid" file is used to keep track of extra plugin process ids and utilities. Now that we have completely setup the UE, next we need to jump to the "igw" which is internet gateway, to download and run the MLP classifier algorithm. "igw" was chosen by typing CTRL and B then 7. Next, a new terminal was created by typing CTRL and B then by typing SHIFT and '. Then we downloaded and extracted the MLP python script to "/opt/webtaskclassifier/" folder. Next, we went to home terminal by typing "cd". Then we executed the following commands to run the MLP classifier.

"ip netns exec igw bash"

"cd /opt/webtaskclassifier/main/"

"python3 live_trained_NN.py"

Results after these steps have shown down.

```
23-Nov-2019 09:43:06.741 automatic empty zone: 9.E.F.IP6.ARPA
23-Nov-2019 09:43:06.741 automatic empty zone: A.E.F.IP6.ARPA
23-Nov-2019 09:43:06.741 automatic empty zone: B.E.F.IP6.ARPA
23-Nov-2019 09:43:06.741 automatic empty zone: 8.B.D.0.1.0.0.2.IP6.ARPA
23-Nov-2019 09:43:06.741 automatic empty zone: EMPTY.AS112.ARPA
23-Nov-2019 09:43:06.743 configuring command channel from '/etc/bind/rndc.key'
23-Nov-2019 09:43:06.743 couldn't add command channel 127.0.0.1#953: file not found
23-Nov-2019 09:43:06.743 configuring command channel from '/etc/bind/rndc.key'
23-Nov-2019 09:43:06.743 couldn't add command channel ::1#953: file not found
23-Nov-2019 09:43:06.743 not using config file logging statement for logging due to -g option
23-Nov-2019 09:43:06.743 managed-keys-zone: loaded serial 4
23-Nov-2019 09:43:06.744 zone 0.in-addr.arpa/IN: loaded serial 1
23-Nov-2019 09:43:06.746 zone 127.in-addr.arpa/IN: loaded serial 1
23-Nov-2019 09:43:06.747 zone 255.in-addr.arpa/IN: loaded serial 1
23-Nov-2019 09:43:06.747 zone localhost/IN: loaded serial 2
23-Nov-2019 09:43:06.747 zone o5gc.mnc001.mcc001.3gppnetwork.org/IN: loaded serial 1418218615
23-Nov-2019 09:43:06.747 all zones loaded
23-Nov-2019 09:43:06.747 running
23-Nov-2019 09:43:06.748 connection refused resolving './DNSKEY/IN': 192.168.254.2#53
23-Nov-2019 09:43:06.748 connection refused resolving './NS/IN': 192.168.254.2#53
23-Nov-2019 09:43:06.748 connection refused resolving 'B.ROOT-SERVERS.NET/AAAA/IN': 192.168.254.2#53
23-Nov-2019 09:43:06.748 connection refused resolving 'E.ROOT-SERVERS.NET/AAAA/IN': 192.168.254.2#53
23-Nov-2019 09:43:06.748 connection refused resolving 'G.ROOT-SERVERS.NET/AAAA/IN': 192.168.254.2#53
23-Nov-2019 09:43:06.749 connection refused resolving 'C.ROOT-SERVERS.NET/AAAA/IN': 192.168.254.2#53
23-Nov-2019 09:43:07.291  validating ./DNSKEY: unable to find a DNSKEY which verifies the DNSKEY RRset and also matches a trusted ke
y for '.'
23-Nov-2019 09:43:07.291 broken trust chain resolving './NS/IN': 202.12.27.33#53

root@test-All-Series:/opt/UCT/Open5GCoreRel.3/phoenix/tools/ph_init# cd
root@test-All-Series:~# ip netns exec igw bash
root@test-All-Series:~# cd /opt/webtaskclassifier/main/
root@test-All-Series:/opt/webtaskclassifier/main# python3 live_trained_NN.py
/usr/local/lib/python3.5/dist-packages/tensorflow/python/framework/dtypes.py:493: FutureWarning: Passing (type, 1) or '1type' as a sy
nonym of type is deprecated; in a future version of numpy, it will be understood as (type, (1,)) / '(1,)type'.
  _np_qint8 = np.dtype([("qint8", np.int8, 1)])
/usr/local/lib/python3.5/dist-packages/tensorflow/python/framework/dtypes.py:494: FutureWarning: Passing (type, 1) or '1type' as a sy
nonym of type is deprecated; in a future version of numpy, it will be understood as (type, (1,)) / '(1,)type'.
  _np_quint8 = np.dtype([("quint8", np.uint8, 1)])
/usr/local/lib/python3.5/dist-packages/tensorflow/python/framework/dtypes.py:495: FutureWarning: Passing (type, 1) or '1type' as a sy
nonym of type is deprecated; in a future version of numpy, it will be understood as (type, (1,)) / '(1,)type'.
  _np_qint16 = np.dtype([("qint16", np.int16, 1)])
/usr/local/lib/python3.5/dist-packages/tensorflow/python/framework/dtypes.py:496: FutureWarning: Passing (type, 1) or '1type' as a sy
nonym of type is deprecated; in a future version of numpy, it will be understood as (type, (1,)) / '(1,)type'.
  _np_quint16 = np.dtype([("quint16", np.uint16, 1)])
/usr/local/lib/python3.5/dist-packages/tensorflow/python/framework/dtypes.py:497: FutureWarning: Passing (type, 1) or '1type' as a sy
nonym of type is deprecated; in a future version of numpy, it will be understood as (type, (1,)) / '(1,)type'.
  _np_qint32 = np.dtype([("qint32", np.int32, 1)])
/usr/local/lib/python3.5/dist-packages/tensorflow/python/framework/dtypes.py:502: FutureWarning: Passing (type, 1) or '1type' as a sy
nonym of type is deprecated; in a future version of numpy, it will be understood as (type, (1,)) / '(1,)type'.
  np_resource = np.dtype([("resource", np.ubyte, 1)])
2019-11-23 11:23:50.962485: I tensorflow/core/platform/cpu_feature_guard.cc:137] Your CPU supports instructions that this TensorFlow
binary was not compiled to use: SSE4.1 SSE4.2 AVX AVX2 FMA
YouTube,
YouTube,
```

Figure 6-10: Starting the Web-Task Classifier at Internet Gateway

Now that we have successfully set up the UE and Internet gateway with MLP classifier. We connected to the browser and conducted experiments.

6.2.2 Getting Results from Zabbix.

After installing Zabbix we can access the Zabbix GUI by typing "https://localhost/Zabbix". Then it will request to enter the User name and the Password as shown in Figure 6-11.

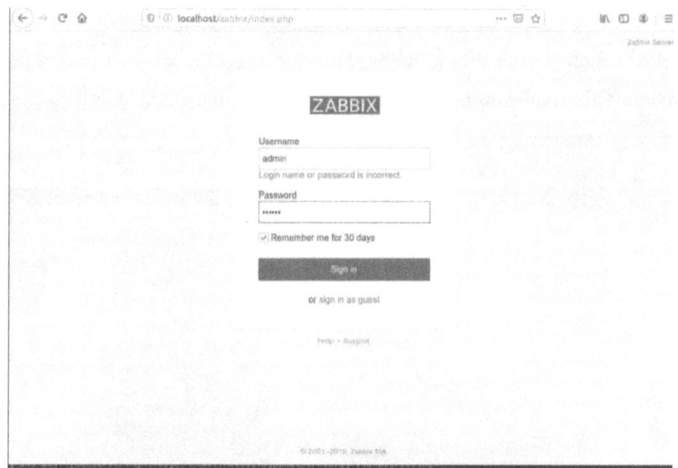

Figure 6-11: Loging in to Zabbix

Once logged in the next step is to setup the host IP. This can be setup selecting "Configurations" and then by selecting "Hosts" tab. Next by clicking the IP address, Host IP was entered.

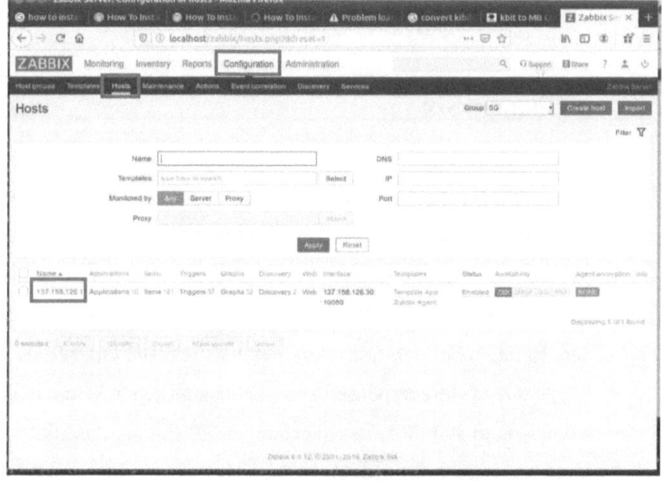

Figure 6-12: Configuring Zabbix

After setting the host IPs, it is possible to see the graph by selecting the "Monitoring" tab and then by selecting the "Graph" tab as shown below. Then the correct graph was chosen from the graph drop-down menu. This graph was used in the results section to explain QoS behaviour.

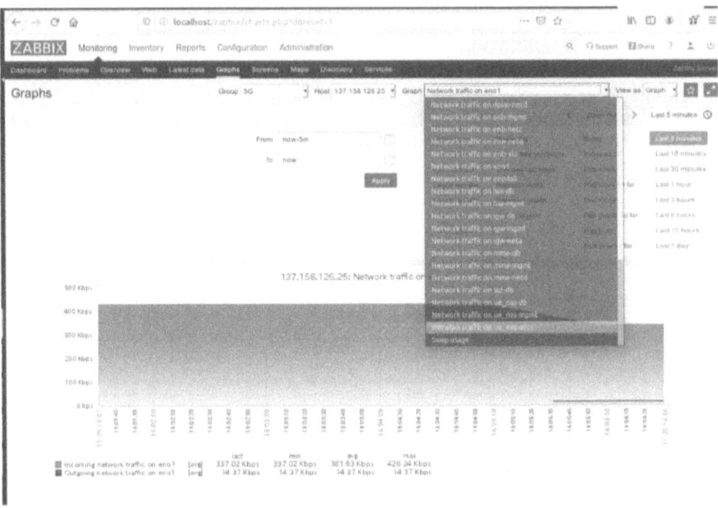

Figure 6-13: Zabbix Graph

6.3 Summary of Chapter Six

Implementation of Open Baton 5G slices and Open5G Core slices discussed in this chapter. First a small background about Open Baton was given. Then the Open Baton architecture was discussed with the main components. Auto Scaling Engine (ASE) is found to be the main component that enables slicing and scaling of each slice based on the web-task. Next, the Open-stack architecture used to combine Open Baton with web-task classifier was shown. Open Baton limited the experiments only to Skype due to slow response. After that using Open5G Core to develop slices was discussed. An introduction to 3GPPP 5G architecture with Web-task classifier was explained. Next the executed commands were explained. Here, the web-task classifier is downloaded to 5G Core's internet gateway. Finally, setting up Zabbix to monitor the bandwidth was explained.

7 RESULT AND DISCUSSION

7.1 Offline & Online Classifier Results

The Table 7-1 shows the connections that were used to collect offline testing data samples with the number of samples. The TCP error bitrate of the testing set is 9.8 times higher than the trained data set. It shows how poor the Wi-Fi network that was used to gather the testing data. Data that was used for the analysis process was collected by using the University of Cape Town network. But the tested data set was collected from a normal ADSL line. Both the data was collected on windows 10 machines.

Web task	Connection Type	No. of Test Samples	No. of Correct Predictions	Recognition percentage (%)
YouTube Video	Wi-Fi	40	40	100
Facebook Video	Wi-Fi	40	38	95
Skype Voice Call	Wi-Fi	40	36	90
Skype Video Call	Wi-Fi	40	39	97
WhatsApp Call	Wi-Fi	40	38	95

Table 7-1: Offline MLP Results

The Table 7-1 shows the Neural Network's predicted results. The Neural Network was able to identify with a 95.50 % accuracy (If we consider the highest degree). Skype shows the lowest accuracy. However, the results prove the robustness of the algorithm and how good the features extracted in the Feature Extraction section.

For the online experiments, the algorithm was activated for an hour while performing web-tasks. However, WhatsApp was not tested due to the lack of equipment available in the lab. MLP output graph was given in Appendix 1.

Web task	Activated duration	Accuracy (%)
YouTube Video	1 hour	99.7
Facebook Video	1 hour	98.6
Skype Voice Call	1 hour	97.7
Skype Video Call	1 hour	83.6

Table 7-2: Online MLP Results

7.2 Online Open Baton Results

A generated slice results for Skype has shown down. For the experiment, we made a skype voice call and used it for five minutes. Then turned ON the skype video calling of the user's PC then after about two minutes turned ON the Skype camera of the other end. After about five minutes turned OFF both ends cameras. Thus making the connection a Skype voice call. Meanwhile we captured the Zabbix output graph. Figure 7-1 shows the captured Zabbix graph. Y-axis of the graph shows the bitrate and the X-axis shows the time. Outgoing IP traffic is shown in blue colour and the incoming IP traffic is shown in green colour.

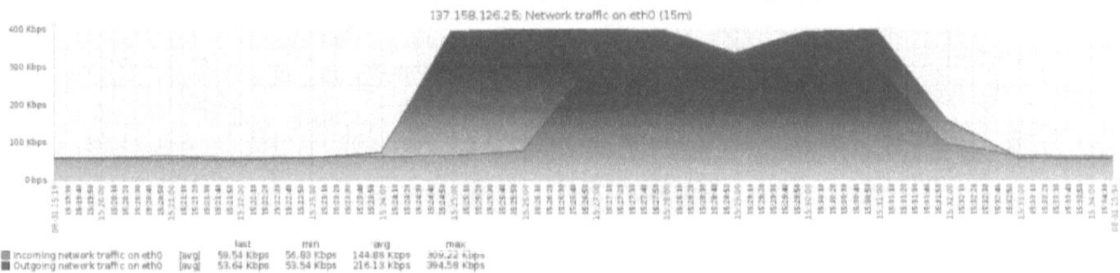

Figure 7-1: Skype Audio Video Zabbix Graph

The following ML output graph's (Figure 7-2) Y-axis shows the one-hot output value of MLP output layer and the X-axis shows the time in Seconds. Since, MLP output was read every 8 seconds, X-axis value 10 means 80 seconds (8 x 10) in real time.

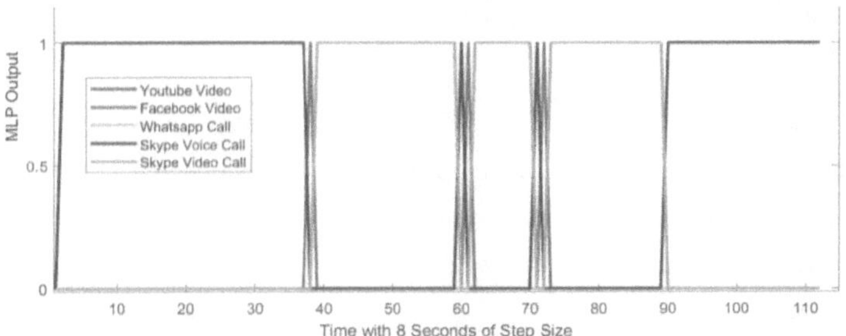

Figure 7-2: Skype Video Audio Real-time Results

According to the Zabbix graph and MLP output graph (Figure 7-2); it is clear that MLP has classified the traffic as Skype voice call within first five minutes ((5 x 60)/8 = 37.5 purple line is one till about 37.5 in Figure 7-2) and then Open Baton has maintained the limited bandwidth allocated for the Skype voice calling which is 0.15 Mbps. According to the graph generated by MLP, it is clear that MLP classifier detected that it is a Skype video call as soon as switched ON the user's webcam. If one notices the blue area of the graph, it is clear that Open Baton orchestrator has changed the QoS to 1 Mbps which allowed more traffic to flow. This proves that Open Baton has read the classifier results as it changes from Skype voice to Skype video. However, there is a delay of 50 Seconds have shown on the graph generated by the Zabbix which needs to be studied. The result of switching ON the camera from the other end after about two minutes is clearly visible on the graph if you notice the increase of receiving bitrate (green area) of the graph. Around 90 eight-second steps, the MLP graph (Figure 7-2) shows the immediate detection of web-task as Skype voice call (due to turning OFF both the Skype cameras after 5 minutes). The gradual drop of sent and received area of Zabbix graph shows the setting back the Skype voice call QoS to the allocated slice.

According to Zabbix graph (Figure 7-1); it is visible that there is a slight decrease in the bandwidth after about 20 seconds from turning ON the second camera. The reason for that can be found in the ML output graph.   Classifier generated two wrong results (around 71 of Figure 7-2) which caused a slight decrease in the QoS.

7.3   Online Open5G Core Results

Results of using Open5G Core to set QoS for Facebook video watching and YouTube video watching are shown in Figure 7-3 and Figure 7-4. An experiment was carried out by watching a YouTube video for about 2 minutes and then watching a video on Facebook for about 5 minutes and then watching a video on YouTube for about 5 minutes. Captured the Zabbix output graph shown in Figure 7-3.

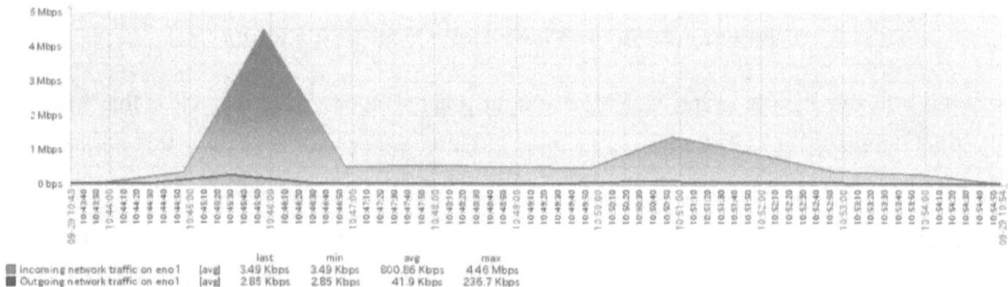

Figure 7-3: Zabbix Graph for Switching Between Facebook Video and YouTube Video

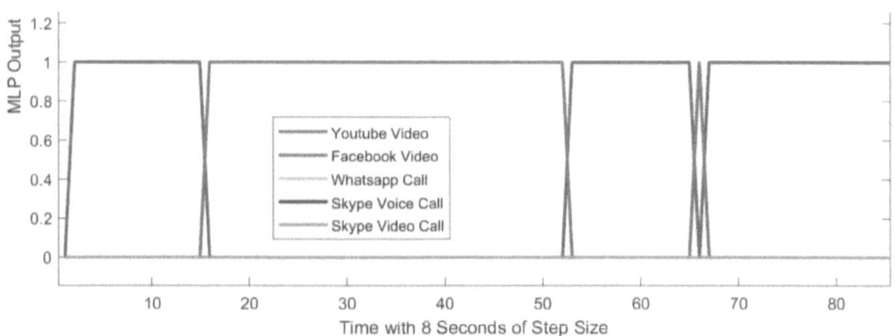

Figure 7-4: MLP Real-time Results for Switching Between Facebook Video and YouTube Video

YouTube video traffic from 10:43 to 10:45 (in Figure 7-3) was successfully detected by the MLP algorithm and it is shown on the MLP output graph (Figure 7-4) from 1 to 15. Then there is a rise (which is about 4.5 Mbps, shows that the bandwidth limit of YouTube which is 2 Mbps has changed) of incoming packet traffic due to caching of the Facebook video. After caching, from about 10:47 to 10:50 a constant amount of traffic has been generated due to constant buffering of Facebook. During these 5 minutes (While caching and buffering) MLP algorithm has successfully detected the web-task and it is visible on the graph (Figure 7-4) from 15 to about 53. Finally, switched from Facebook video to YouTube video around 10:50 (Figure 7-3). Thus there is a packet traffic rise in the Zabbix graph (Figure 7-3) is visible due to caching of YouTube video. However, this rise is less than 2 Mbps which shows that the bandwidth limit for YouTube video has maintained. Then YouTube video was watched for 5 minutes and these 5 minutes were shown on the MLP output graph (Figure 7-4) from 53 to about 85. Within these 5 minutes, there is a misclassification around 66 due to the pause caused while changing from one video to another video on YouTube.

Results of switching from Skype Voice Call to YouTube video are shown in Figure 7-5 and Figure 7-6. In this experiment, a Skype Voice Call was made for about 5 minutes and then switched to a YouTube Video for 5 minutes. Bitrate pattern generated by Skype Voice Call and YouTube video is shown in Figure 7-5.

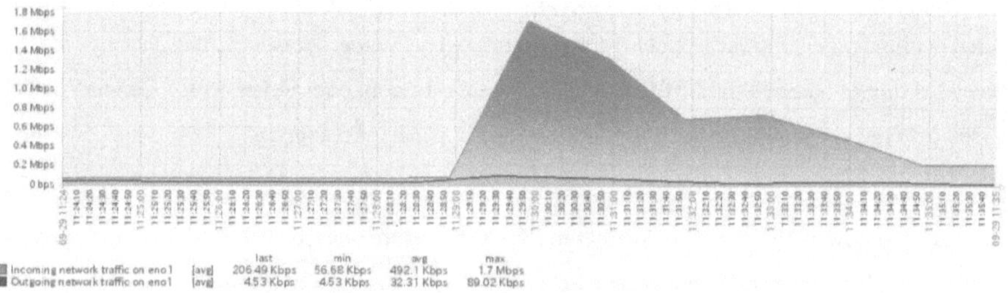

Figure 7-5: Zabbix Graph for Switching Between Skype Voice Call and YouTube Video

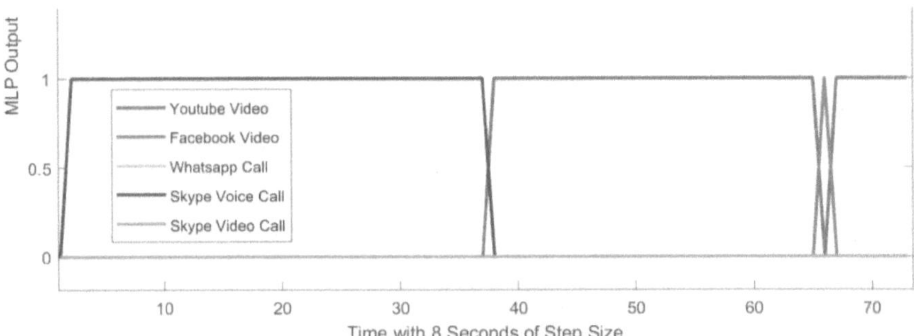

Figure 7-6: MLP Output Results for Switching Between Skype Voice Call and YouTube Video

We started the web-task classifier algorithm after making a Skype voice call. Thus, the MLP output graph (Figure 7-6) starts with Skype voice call. On the Zabbix graph (Figure 7-5), the Skype voice call was shown from 11:24 to 11:29 and corresponding MLP output can be seen from 1 to 38. During this period, the data rate has maintained a value less than the allowed bandwidth, which is 0.15 Mbps. After 11:29 a YouTube video was watched. Thus, there is high incoming traffic due to caching process of YouTube. One misclassification has occurred while watching YouTube. If one notices the Zabbix graph (Figure 7-5), it is clear that there is a big bandwidth difference when switching from Skype Voice Call to YouTube Video because of the data requirement to watch a video without interruption is much higher compared to voice. However, the data rate has not exceeded the set bandwidth (2 Mbps). In a conventional setup, both Skype Voice Call to YouTube Video gets the same amount of bandwidth which is a waste of resources.

Skype Voice Call to Skype Video call switching (the same experiment carried with Open Baton) was tested below with Open5G Core setup. Same as before started with a Skype voice call and after about 4 minutes user's cam was switched ON. Next, after about 2 minutes the camera on the other side was switched ON. Then continued the experiment for about 4 minutes with both the cameras ON.

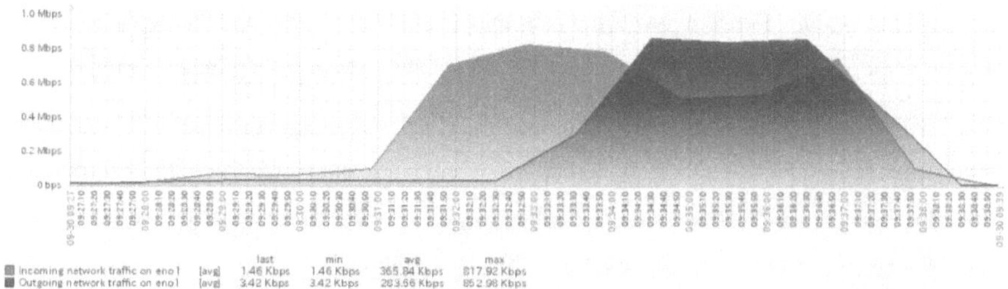

Figure 7-7: Zabbix Graph for Switching Between Skype Voice Call and Skype Video Call

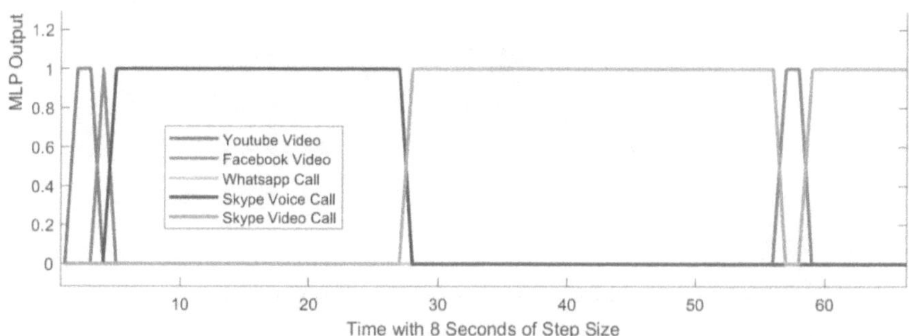

Figure 7-8: MLP Output Graph for Switching Between Skype Voice Call and Skype Video Call

A Skype voice call was made at 09:27 (Figure 7-7) and it has been identified by the MLP algorithm around 4 (Figure 7-8) then classifier has identified the web-task without any misclassification. Next, when user camera was ON around 09:31 the classifier has successfully switched from voice to video around 29 in Figure 7-8. Identification as a video call even when one camera is ON depicts the robustness of the algorithm. Turning ON the camera on the other side can be seen on the Zabbix graph around 09:32:30 (Figure 7-7). However, there are two misclassifications around 57 on MLP output graph. The bandwidth limits were followed through the time periods according to web-tasks as in previous experiments.

QoS settings (Table 6-1) for the above experiments are to give good user experience (user can watch HD quality videos, Skype calls without any lagging, etc.), thus hard to observe the bandwidth limitations. Hence to prove the concept of bandwidth limiting, a Skype video call was made for about 15 minutes and then changed the download and upload traffic bandwidth.

Started with 0.46Mbps inbound bandwidth and 0.92Mbps outbound bandwidth and after about 6 minutes changed the bandwidth limits to 0.92Mbps inbound bandwidth and 0.46Mbps outbound bandwidth. This is clearly visible in the Zabbix graph (Figure 7-9) given bellow as the usage of bandwidth switching in the middle around 12:39:30. Inbound traffic was kept around 0.46Mbps for the first 6 minutes (from around12.34.00 to 12.40.00 in the Figure 7-9) and then outbound traffic was limited to around 0.46Mbps for the remaining time.

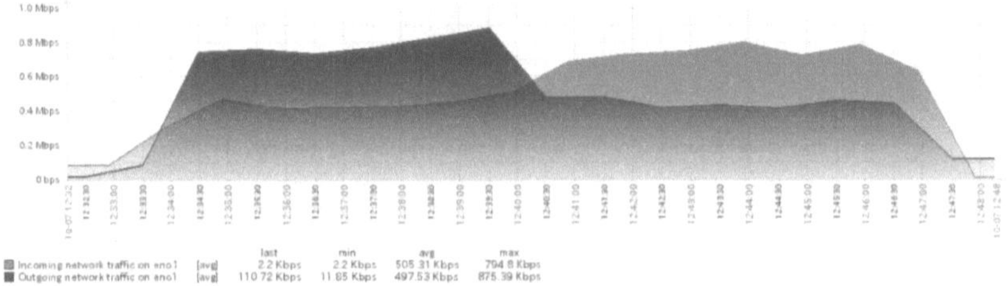

Figure 7-9: Skype Video Call with Different QoS Settings

We also tested the algorithm for low bandwidths. Results of the following table have been attached in Appendix 1.

Web Task	QoS (Bandwidth) in Mbps
YouTube Video	1.50
Facebook Video	1.50
Skype Voice Call	0.075
Skype Video Call	0.50

Table 7-3: Low Bandwidth Settings

Unfortunately unable to get real-time analysis for WhatsApp due to technical issues of testbed but all the other web tasks were tested and clearly observed that the algorithm is successfully classifying and setting the QoS limits.

7.4 Summary of Chapter Seven

Results of the algorithm were discussed in this chapter. First, the offline and online results of web-task classifier was explained. According to offline results, YouTube video watching was recognized with an accuracy of 100% and for the online test both YouTube video watching and Skype voice calls were recognized with an 97.7% accuracy. Next Open Baton online bandwidth results were explained for Skype Video and Skype Voice calling. Due to sluggish response of Openstack architecture, live testing was limited just for Skype Video and Skype Voice. Then Open5G Core live experiment results were discussed. Bandwidth graphs generated by Open5G Core proved that the algorithm is successfully slicing web-tasks. Finally, we tested the algorithm under low bandwidth conditions.

8 Conclusions and Future Work

In this study, we have considered a unique algorithm, which can develop ultra-slices based on the context of the network. The algorithm is a combination of 5G orchestrator and web-task finger printing (WTFP). An MLP NN was used after considering CNN, RNN and SVM to identify different application tasks, namely YouTube Video, Facebook Video, WhatsApp Call, Skype Voice Call and Skype Video Call. High accuracy achieved by the algorithm shows the quality of work done during the feature identification and extraction. After classification, Open Baton and Open5G Core were used to generate a 5G ultra-slice.

MLP NN performed better than CNN due to manual feature extraction. In this case, MLP outperformed CNN by about 9.63 % and RNN by 2.92 % and SVM by 0.97%. Another noticeable outcome of the study is that using sigmoid function as activation increased the accuracy by about 0.97%.

The encryption, protocol, resolution (for videos), device, network type independent algorithm was developed, by considering 5 seconds of data flow. 5 seconds was found to be the best minimum time window after reducing it from a minute of dataflow. A larger window sizes such as 30 Seconds, 1 Minute gave better classification results. We observed that the operating system used on the machine affecting the packet length histogram data patterns. Thus, the accuracy was dropped when using Ubuntu. However, including training sets from the Ubuntu machine helped to increase the accuracy.

The algorithm proves that this method can be applied to any web-task that a person wants to identify as long as he can filter the necessary data from the packet length histogram. The number of web-task can be increased by cascading NNs as shown in previous work [69]. However, human interaction is required when initially adding a new web-task for the algorithm.

The Open Baton 5G orchestrator successfully generated ultra-slices based on predefined QoS, which helped to give the best user experience for the tested five web tasks. Testing was done with Open 5G Core also proves the ability to generate ultra-slices based on web-task to improve the user experience in the mobile core network.

When comparing the QoS settings of Table 6-1 and Table 7-3 it is visible that the overall bandwidth has been reduced by half. This proves that the algorithm performs even with low bandwidths conditions. Thus, this algorithm can be used to allocate bandwidth in the 5G Core Network when there is an emergency in the network. However, when comparing results of Table 6-1 and Table 7-3 there is a slight drop of accuracy. It is not significant, and it can be solved by including data samples of low bandwidth settings to the training set.

In future work, we intend to utilise the algorithm to develop a system which can use maximum bandwidth in a more efficient way in the 5G Network. However, automating the feature selection process will also help to increase the robustness of the algorithm.

In this study, a single slice has been developed and modified to cater each web-tasks. This algorithm will also be used in multiple slices to get the maximum benefit of the algorithm.

REFERENCES

[1] "Number of available applications in the google play store," [Online]. Available: http://www.statista.com/statistics/266210/number-of-available-applications-in-the-google-play-st ore/..

[2] "The METIS 2020 Project – Laying the foundation of 5G," [Online]. Available: https://metis2020.com/.

[3] "Next Generation Mobile Networks (NGMN)," [Online]. Available: https://www.ngmn.org/.

[4] "The 5G Infrastructure Public Private Partnership (5G PPP)," [Online]. Available: https://5g-ppp.eu/white-papers/.

[5] "The Voice of 5G and LTE for the Americas," [Online]. Available: www.5gamericas.org/.

[6] "International Mobile Telecommunications-2020," [Online]. Available: www.imt-2020.org.cn/en/.

[7] "Fifth Generation Mobile Communication Promotion Forum," [Online]. Available: https://5gmf.jp/en/.

[8] "ITU," [Online]. Available: https://www.itu.int/.

[9] "Focus Group on IMT-2020," [Online]. Available: https://www.itu.int/en/ITU-T/focusgroups/imt-2020/Pages/default.aspx.

[10] "5G Network Architecture 5G Network Architecture - Huawei," [Online]. Available: https://www.huawei.com/minisite/hwmbbf16/insights/5G-Nework-Architecture-Whitepaper-en.pdf.

[11] A. Nakao, "End-to-end Network Slicing for 5G Mobile Networks," *journal of information processing,* pp. 153-163, 2017.

[12] "5G Mobile Communications Systems for 2020 and Beyond," [Online]. Available: https://5gmf.jp/wp/wp-content/uploads/2016/09/5GMF.

[13] "Open Baton," [Online]. Available: https://openbaton.github.io/.

[14] H. Bacic, "Are You Using A Content Delivery Network For Your Website Yet? You Should Be," AllBusiness , [Online]. Available: https://www.forbes.com/sites/allbusiness/2015/03/16/are-you-using-a-content-delivery-network-for-your-website-yet-you-should-be/#2273f375449e.

[15] P. Warren, C. Boldyreff and M. Munro, "The evolution of Websites," in *Proceedings Seventh International Workshop on Program Comprehension*, 1999.

[16] T. Bujlow, V. Carela-Español and P. Barlet-Ros, "Independent comparison of popular DPI tools for traffic classification," *Computer Networks,* vol. 76, pp. 75-89, 2015.

[17] J. Garcia, "A clustering-based analysis of DPI-labeled video flow characteristics in cellular networks," in *2017 IFIP/IEEE Symposium on Integrated Network and Service Management (IM)*, 2017.

[18] J. Kampeas, A. Cohen and O. Gurewitz, "Traffic Classification Based on Zero-Length Packets," *IEEE Transactions on Network and Service Management,* vol. 15, pp. 1049-1062, 9 2018.

[19] V. F. Taylor, R. Spolaor, M. Conti and P. 6. -. 7. Ivan Martinovic Robust Smartphone App Identification via Encrypted Network Traffic Analysis IEEE Transactions on Information Forensics and Security Volume: 13.

[20] M. Liberatore and B. N. Levine, "Inferring the Source of Encrypted HTTP Connections," in *Proceedings of the 13th ACM Conference on Computer and Communications Security*, New York, NY, USA, 2006.

[21] A. Hintz, "Fingerprinting Websites Using Traffic Analysis," in *Proceedings of the 2Nd International Conference on Privacy Enhancing Technologies*, Berlin, 2003.

[22] Q. Sun, D. R. Simon, Y.-M. Wang, W. Russell, V. N. Padmanabhan and L. Qiu, "Statistical identification of encrypted Web browsing traffic," in *Proceedings 2002 IEEE Symposium on Security and Privacy*, 2002.

[23] T. Stöber, M. Frank, J. Schmitt and I. Martinovic, "Who Do You Sync You Are?: Smartphone Fingerprinting via Application Behaviour," in *Proceedings of the Sixth ACM Conference on Security and Privacy in Wireless and Mobile Networks*, New York, NY, USA, 2013.

[24] Q. Wang, A. Yahyavi, B. Kemme and W. He, "I know what you did on your smartphone: Inferring app usage over encrypted data traffic," in *2015 IEEE Conference on Communications and Network Security (CNS)*, 2015.

[25] G. Aceto, D. Ciuonzo, A. Montieri and A. Pescape, "Traffic Classification of Mobile Apps through Multi-Classification," in *GLOBECOM 2017 - 2017 IEEE Global Communications Conference*, 2017.

[26] S. Rezaei, B. Kroencke and X. Liu, "Large-scale Mobile App Identification Using Deep Learning," *IEEE Access 8 ,* pp. 348-362, 2019.

[27] I. Alawe, A. Ksentini, Y. Hadjadj-Aoul and P. Bertin, "Improving Traffic Forecasting for 5G Core Network Scalability: A Machine Learning Approach," *IEEE Network,* vol. 32, pp. 42-49, 11 2018.

[28] R. Ferrus, O. Sallent, J. Perez-Romero and R. Agusti, "On 5G Radio Access Network Slicing: Radio Interface Protocol Features and Configuration," in *IEEE Communications Magazine*, 2018.

[29] C. Politis, K. Liolis, M. Corici, E. Troudt, Z. Szabó and J. Cahill, "Design of Moving Experimentation Facility to Showcase Satellite Integration into 5G," in *2019 European Conference on Networks and Communications (EuCNC)*, 2019.

[30] M. Corici, T. SandraBuda, R. Shrestha, E. Cau, T. Metin and H. Assem, "Practical Performance Degradation Mitigation Solution Using Anomaly Detection for Carrier-Grade

Software Networks," in *2018 IEEE Conference on Standards for Communications and Networking (CSCN)*, 2018.

[31] R. Casellas, R. Martínez, L. Velasco, R. Vilalta, P. Pavón, D. O. King and R. Muñoz, "Enabling Data Analytics and Machine Learning for 5G Services within Disaggregated Multi-Layer Transport Networks," *2018 20th International Conference on Transparent Optical Networks (ICTON)*, pp. 1-4, 2018.

[32] V. P. Kafle, Y. Fukushima, P. Martinez-Julia and T. Miyazawa, "Consideration On Automation of 5G Network Slicing with Machine Learning," in *2018 ITU Kaleidoscope: Machine Learning for a 5G Future (ITU K)*, 2018.

[33] A. Nakao, "Application specific slicing for MVNO through software-defined data plane enhancing SDN," in *2016 Optical Fiber Communications Conference and Exhibition (OFC)*, 2016.

[34] A. Nakao and P. Du, "Application-specific slicing for MVNO and traffic characterization [Invited]," *IEEE/OSA Journal of Optical Communications and Networking*, vol. 9, pp. A256-A262, 2 2017.

[35] S. Blitz, "What Is Exploratory Data Analysis?," [Online]. Available: https://www.sisense.com/blog/exploratory-data-analysis/ .

[36] "Max IP Packet Size," [Online]. Available: https://community.cisco.com/t5/switching/max-ip-packet-size/td-p/1019561.

[37] "Maximum transmission uni.," Wikipedia, [Online]. Available: https://en.wikipedia.org/wiki/Maximum_transmission_uni..

[38] D. Herrmann, R. Wendolsky and H. Federrath, "Website Fingerprinting: Attacking Popular Privacy Enhancing Technologies with the Multinomial NaïVe-bayes Classifier," in *Proceedings of the 2009 ACM Workshop on Cloud Computing Security*, New York, NY, USA, 2009.

[39] S. Patel, "Machine Learning 101," medium, 3 May 2017. [Online]. Available: https://medium.com/machine-learning-101/chapter-2-svm-support-vector-machine-theory-f0812effc72.

[40] B. Stecanella, "An introduction to Support Vector Machines (SVM)," no. https://monkeylearn.com/blog/introduction-to-support-vector-machines-svm/, 2017 .

[41] T. Fletcher, "Support Vector Machines Explained," UCL, 23 December 2008. [Online]. Available: www.cs.ucl.ac.uk/staff/T.Fletcher/. [Accessed 25 July 2019].

[42] L. Wang, "Support Vector Machines: Theory and Applications," NTU, 2005 . [Online]. Available: https://www.ntu.edu.sg/home/elpwang/PDF_web/05_SVM_basic.pdf.

[43] N. R. E. W. C. L. José C. Príncipe, Neural and adaptive systems: fundamentals through simulations, Wiley, 2000.

[44] S. Raschka, "Single-Layer Neural Networks and Gradient Descent," sebastianraschka, 24 03 2015. [Online]. Available: https://sebastianraschka.com/Articles/2015_singlelayer_neurons.html.

[45] "Understanding CNNs (from Stanford's CS231n course)," Stanford University , [Online]. Available: http://cs231n.github.io/convolutional-networks/#conv.

[46] T. Acharya, Image Processing Principles and Applications, A John Wiley & Sons.

[47] A. Dertat, "Applied Deep Learning - Part 4: Convolutional Neural Networks," 8 November 2017. [Online]. Available: https://towardsdatascience.com/applied-deep-learning-part-4-convolutional-neural-networks-584bc134c1e2.

[48] J. Yung, "Explaining Tensorflow Code for a Convolutional Neural Network," May 2017. [Online]. Available: http://www.jessicayung.com/explaining-tensorflow-code-for-a-convolutional-neural-network/.

[49] "Convolutional Neural Networks," [Online]. Available: http://cs231n.github.io/convolutional-networks/#conv. [Accessed 30 07 2019].

[50] "Understanding LSTM Networks," 27 August 2015. [Online]. Available: http://colah.github.io/posts/2015-08-Understanding-LSTMs/.

[51] J. Chhabra, "Understanding LSTM in Tensorflow (MNIST dataset)," [Online]. Available: https://jasdeep06.github.io/posts/Understanding-LSTM-in-Tensorflow-MNIST/.

[52] S. Banerjee, "An Introduction to Recurrent Neural Networks," Medium, 23 May 2018. [Online]. Available: https://medium.com/explore-artificial-intelligence/an-introduction-to-recurrent-neural-networks-72c97bf0912.

[53] "Radial basis function kernel," Wikipedia, [Online]. Available: https://en.wikipedia.org/wiki/Radial_basis_function_kernel.

[54] "Network Function Virtualization Management and Orchestration," ETSI NFV, [Online]. Available: https://www.etsi.org/deliver/etsi_gs/NFV-MAN/001_099/001/01.01.01_60/gs_NFV-MAN001v010101p.pdf.

[55] G. E. Dmitriy Andrushko, "What is the best NFV Orchestration platform? A review of OSM, Open-O, CORD, and Cloudify," 8 March 2017. [Online]. Available: https://www.mirantis.com/blog/which-nfv-orchestration-platform-best-review-osm-open-o-cord-cloudify/. [Accessed 11 August 2019].

[56] "The Open Baton MANO Group Pre-Dates OSM and Open-O," [Online]. Available: https://www.sdxcentral.com/articles/news/open-baton-mano-group-pre-dates-osm-open-o/2017/01/. [Accessed 11 August 2019].

[57] "OSM," [Online]. Available: https://osm.etsi.org/. [Accessed 11 August 2019].

[58] "onap," [Online]. Available: https://www.onap.org/. [Accessed 12 08 2019].

[59] CORD, [Online]. Available: https://opencord.org/. [Accessed 12 August 2019].

[60] Cloudify, [Online]. Available: https://docs.cloudify.co/5.0.0/. [Accessed 12 August 2019].

[61] "Open Baton," Fraunhofer Fokus, [Online]. Available: https://openbaton.github.io/documentation/. [Accessed 12 August 2019].

[62] "RabbitMQ," [Online]. Available: https://www.rabbitmq.com/. [Accessed 13 August 2019].

[63] L. Johansson, "Part 1: RabbitMQ for beginners - What is RabbitMQ?," 18 May 2015. [Online]. Available: https://www.cloudamqp.com/blog/2015-05-18-part1-rabbitmq-for-beginners-what-is-rabbitmq.html.

[64] M. Rouse, "Remote Procedure Call (RPC)," [Online]. Available: https://searchmicroservices.techtarget.com/definition/Remote-Procedure-Call-RPC. [Accessed 15 August 2019].

[65] "Open Stack," [Online]. Available: https://www.openstack.org/. [Accessed 15 August 2019].

[66] "Zabbix," [Online]. Available: http://www.zabbix.com/. [Accessed 15 August 2019].

[67] "Open 5G Core," Fraunhofer FOKUS, [Online]. Available: https://www.open5gcore.org/. [Accessed 09 September 2019].

[68] E. Helix, "5G Service-Based Architecture (SBA)," Medium, 20 October 2018. [Online]. Available: https://medium.com/5g-nr/5g-service-based-architecture-sba-47900b0ded0a. [Accessed 09 September 2019].

[69] M. Rimas, R. P. Thilakumara and P. Koswatta, "Optical character recognition for Sinhala language," in *IEEE Global Humanitarian Technology Conference*, Trivandrum, 2013.

APPENDIX 1

Results of Table 7-2: Online MLP Results.

MLP output for YouTube.

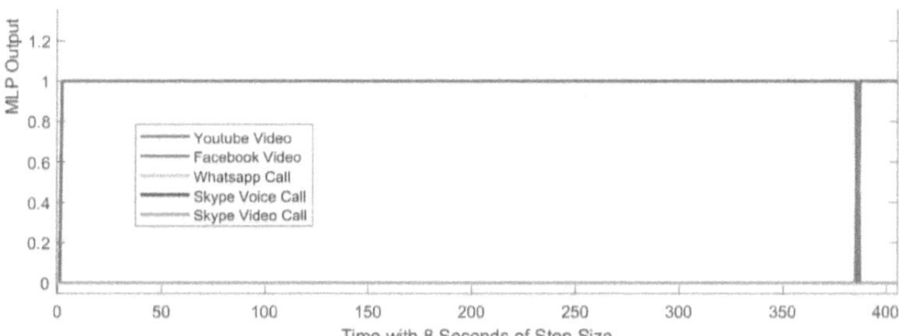

MLP output for Facebook.

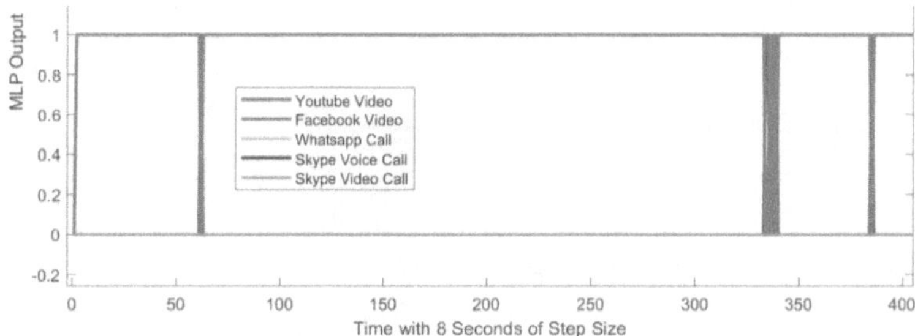

MLP output for Skype Voice Call.

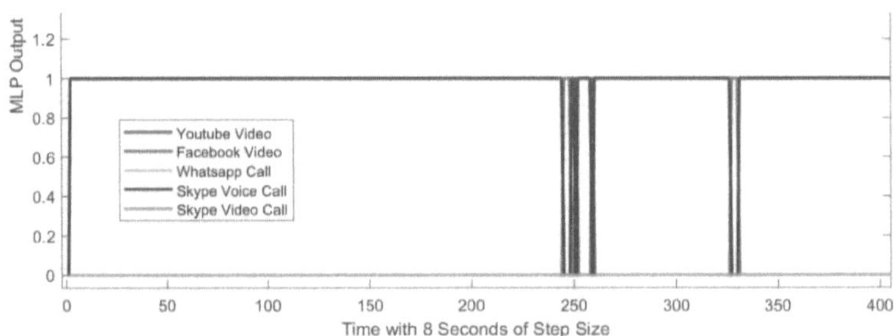

MLP output for Skype Video Call.

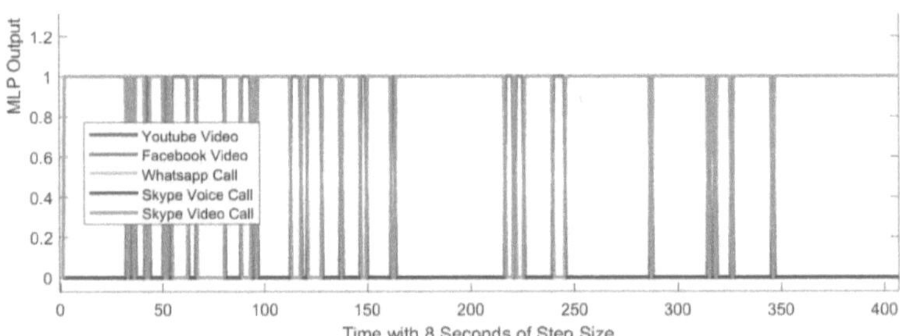

Results of Table 7-3: Low Bandwidth Settings have shown below.

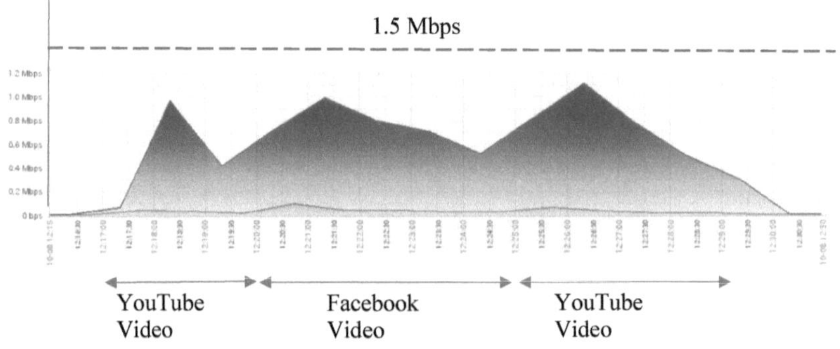

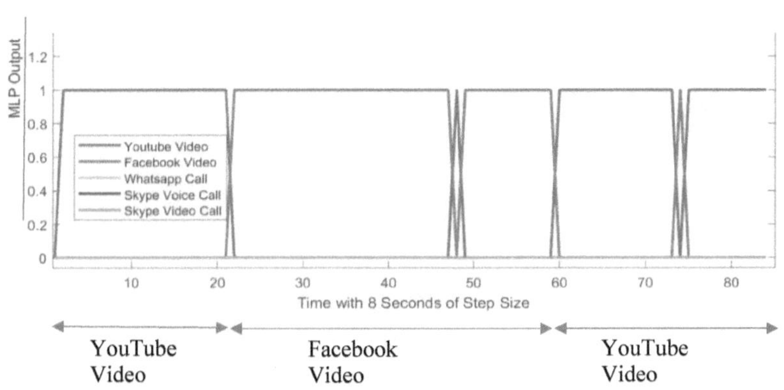

MLP Output
1.2
1
0.8
0.6
0.4
0.2
0
Youtube Video
Facebook Video
Whatsapp Call
Skype Voice Call
Skype Video Call
10
20
30
40
50
60
70
80
Time with 8 Seconds of Step Size
YouTube Video
Facebook Video
YouTube Video

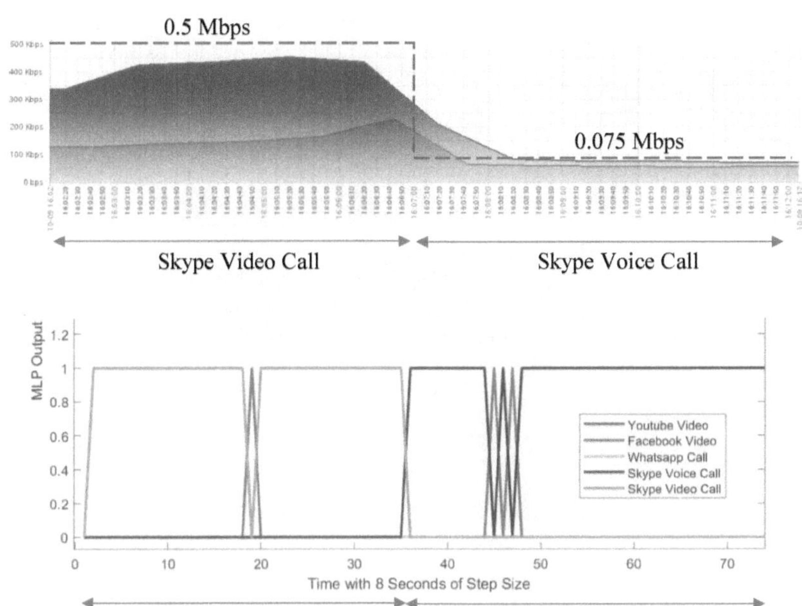

0.5 Mbps
500 Kbps
400 Kbps
300 Kbps
200 Kbps
100 Kbps
0 bps
0.075 Mbps
Skype Video Call
Skype Voice Call

MLP Output
1.2
1
0.8
0.6
0.4
0.2
0
0
10
20
30
40
50
60
70
Time with 8 Seconds of Step Size
Youtube Video
Facebook Video
Whatsapp Call
Skype Voice Call
Skype Video Call
Skype Video Call
Skype Voice Call

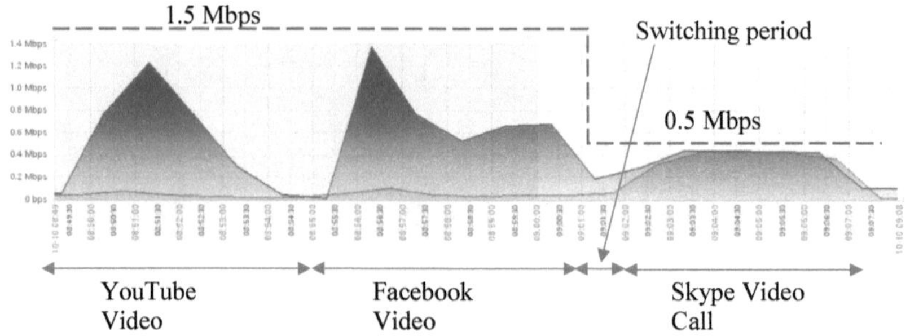

1.5 Mbps
Switching period
0.5 Mbps
1.4 Mbps
1.2 Mbps
1.0 Mbps
0.8 Mbps
0.6 Mbps
0.4 Mbps
0.2 Mbps
0 bps
YouTube
Video
Facebook
Video
Skype Video
Call

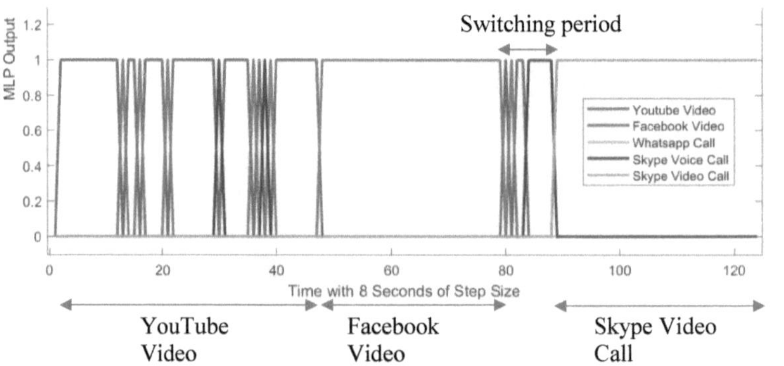

Switching period
MLP Output
1.2
1
0.8
0.6
0.4
0.2
0
Youtube Video
Facebook Video
Whatsapp Call
Skype Voice Call
Skype Video Call
0
20
40
60
80
100
120
Time with 8 Seconds of Step Size
YouTube
Video
Facebook
Video
Skype Video
Call

APPENDIX 2

Possible Use Cases

This algorithm can be used wherever you need to prioritize different web tasks. Hence there are a lot of real-world applications, few of them were shown down.

1. In the near future Shopping mall's internet connection would be in a separate slice. But as we all know that people are using vast amount of applications on their phone, laptops, etc. to give all of the connected people the best available internet experience, it is required to use all the resources. By maintaining a separate slice for main web tasks would help to prioritize necessary web tasks. For example, someone might watch YouTube videos while waiting for another person. Thus giving the best YouTube experience might give a good impression for the shopping mall.

2. Companies can prioritize payments. Imagine a company that deals with online payments, they can develop a separate slice for online payment so that they can pay or get paid without any delay. This can be really useful in Wall Street where they need to access internet without any delay.

3. In a hospital there are certain applications that they want to run without any disturbance, for example some deaf patients need to contact their translator to explain their illness to the doctor. There are some applications that are connecting to internet to translate sign-language. These kind of applications need a separate slice (especially for hospitals in rural areas) so that it can run without any lag.

4. Imagine there is a slice for IPTV so the router connected to TV would be in the IPTV slice but some of the other family members may have connected to the same router thus one might use YouTube, Facebook, etc. but the 5G Orchestrator would not be able to distinguish IPTV users from the normal web user thus end up providing same bandwidth all the time. This is a waste of resources and a waste of bandwidth.

5. Although data was captured at the client's PC in this study, the presented solution can be deployed either as a driver or can be embedded in the home or wireless network routers. Embedding this kind of algorithm in data-plane switches will provide a great advantage when preventing RAN cashing attacks in 5G networks.

6. This algorithm would be useful for network managers as well they can throttle the Facebook video if there is a need to save the network bandwidth for another useful task. Similarly, application developers can use this information for various purposes such as marketing a product below the Facebook video.

The applications of identifying web-task has many use cases beyond the given examples. It is clear that identifying web tasks could help to enhance Internet quality of experience.

APPENDIX 3

The latest trained web-task classifier algorithm link was given below. Note that this algorithm was slightly different (Number of features, Feature index numbers, etc..) from the explained algorithm, because it was trained spsifically for the 5G Core. This code might change as we experiment to improve the algorithm.

https://github.com/onerimas/Final_exe_version_1/tree/master/main

APPENDIX 4

Publications:

- "Using Machine Learning Techniques in Developing an Autonomous Network Orchestration Scheme in 5G Networks", a work in progress paper was published at the Southern Africa Telecommunication Networks and Applications Conference (SATNAC) in 2018 September.
  https://www.researchgate.net/publication/329906358_Using_Machine_Learning_Techniq ues_in_Developing_an_Autonomous_Network_Orchestration_Scheme_in_5G_Networks

- "Developing an AI-based Web Audio and Video Task Classifier for Context Aware Networks", a full paper on web-task classification with offline results was published at the Southern Africa Telecommunication Networks and Applications Conference (SATNAC) in 2019 September.
  https://www.researchgate.net/publication/335661767_Developing_an_AI-based_Web_Audio_and_Video_Task_Classifier_for_Context_Aware_Networks